D0773504

Preventing Identity Theft in Your Business

How to Protect Your Business, Customers, and Employees

Judith M. Collins

John Wiley & Sons, Inc.

This book is printed on acid-free paper. ∞

Copyright © 2005 by John Wiley & Sons, Inc. All rights reserved.

Published by John Wiley & Sons, Inc., Hoboken, New Jersey

Published simultaneously in Canada

No part of this publication may be reproduced, stored in a retrieval system, or transmitted in any form or by any means, electronic, mechanical, photocopying, recording, scanning, or otherwise, except as permitted under Section 107 or 108 of the 1976 United States Copyright Act, without either the prior written permission of the Publisher, or authorization through payment of the appropriate per-copy fee to the Copyright Clearance Center, Inc., 222 Rosewood Drive, Danvers, MA 01923, 978-750-8400, fax 978-646-8600, or on the Web at *www.copyright.com*. Requests to the Publisher for permission should be addressed to the Permissions Department, John Wiley & Sons, Inc., 111 River Street, Hoboken, NJ 07030, 201-748-6011, fax 201-748-6008, e-mail: *permcoordinator@wiley.com*.

Limit of Liability/Disclaimer of Warranty: While the publisher and author have used their best efforts in preparing this book, they make no representations or warranties with respect to the accuracy or completeness of the contents of this book and specifically disclaim any implied warranties of merchantability or fitness for a particular purpose. No warranty may be created or extended by sales representatives or written sales materials. The advice and strategies contained herein may not be suitable for your situation. You should consult with a professional where appropriate. Neither the publisher nor author shall be liable for any loss of profit or any other commercial damages, including but not limited to special, incidental, consequential, or other damages.

For general information on our other products and services, or technical support, please contact our Customer Care Department within the United States at 800-762-2974, outside the United States at 317-572-3993 or fax 317-572-4002.

Wiley also publishes its books in a variety of electronic formats. Some content that appears in print may not be available in electronic books.

Library of Congress Cataloging-in-Publication Data

Collins, Judith M.
  Preventing identity theft in your business : how to protect your business, customers, and employees / Judith M. Collins.
    p. cm.
  Includes index.
  ISBN 0-471-69469-X (cloth)
  1. Identity theft—United States—Prevention. I. Title.
  HV6679.C653 2005
  658.4'72—dc22

                                                        2004022093

Printed in the United States of America

10 9 8 7 6 5 4 3 2 1

To victims of identity theft and employees who help prevent it

ACKNOWLEDGMENTS

More than a faithful colleague and meticulous research assistant, Sandra Hoffman is a valued friend. As associate director, Sandra diligently, skillfully, and solely managed the bustling activities of Identity Theft Crime and Research Lab for three months so that I could write this book. I publicly acknowledge that without Sandra this book would not have been possible. With deep appreciation, I thank you, Sandra.

I also am indebted to my editor at John Wiley & Sons, Tim Burgard. Tim took the time to read my manuscript and recognized its potential importance for businesses. He provided the logistical and organizational support necessary to bring this book to fruition and along the way provided many constructive suggestions for improvements. Moreover, throughout the summer of 2004, Tim routinely and consistently prompted me for the next "batch" (of chapters). Because of Tim, this book moved from "in progress" to "in production." Thank you, Tim, for the guidance you've given me and also for believing with me that this book can positively impact businesses and people.

With appreciation, I especially thank my son, Michael Collins. Michael read every word of every chapter and offered many recommendations for modifications. I made them all. I now find it difficult to adequately express my deep gratitude to Michael, who unselfishly shared with me considerable time and his intellectual talents in reviewing chapter writes and rewrites. Thank you, son, for your invaluable contributions.

And to Larry Collins, my husband, mentor, and enthusiastic supporter of each next "project," thank you for being alongside me throughout these life's adventures.

CONTENTS

PART II: IDENTITY THEFT PREVENTION

PREFACE

All companies that engage in financial transactions are bound by law to establish and enforce information security programs to prevent identity theft. Security "standards" are required by at least five federal laws, including the Fair Credit Reporting Act, the Federal Trade Commission's Privacy Rule, the Banking Guidelines, the Health Insurance Portability and Accountability Act, and the Gramm-Leach-Bliley Safeguards Rule. But there are problems. Nowhere do any of these laws describe how to develop, maintain, and enforce an information security program. In effect, the laws fail to stipulate what constitutes an "information security program" or "standards" for security.

Granted, the laws do specify information technology (IT) security—the security of computers and networks. Indeed, the main theme at the September 2004 American Banking Association's Identity Theft Symposium was "Technology to the Rescue." Bankers were informed of online products and protections and advised to prevent identity theft by using tools such as encryption, authentication, and software programs that guard against email and other computer fraud. *But computers do not steal identities*.

Rather, recent studies indicate that at least 50 percent or more of identity thefts are committed inside the workplace by a dishonest few employees who steal the Social Security, credit card, banking, or other numbers from their coworkers and customers. Federal laws fail, however, to cover *people* within businesses who have access to personal identities and the work *processes* used to manage and maintain such information.

The federal laws fall short. Computer security alone will not work. To secure company borders from the threat of identity theft requires an inclusive and exhaustive three-fold approach to secure people, processes, *and* the IT property. And the techniques used to develop, maintain, and enforce such an information security program would use universally established and widely documented methods known to be reliable and valid and that are inexpensive and accessible for all businesses, large and small. Fortunately, such methods exist and so, therefore, do the security solutions.

Preventing Identity Theft in Your Business shows how employee-manager teams can develop a set of Security Standards using step-by-step instructions written in lay language and using methods from industrial and organizational psychology, the management sciences, and the field of criminal justice. The methods are inexpensive, comprehensive, and universally applicable to all businesses regardless of size, type, or geographic location. Within six months or less, employees and their managers can bring any company into compliance with all current as well as any future-enacted laws.

Preventing Identity Theft in Your Business shows how all companies can build effective corporate policies to protect the identities of employees and their customers without impacting budgets and business operations. What's more, these *Security* Standards incorporate *performance* standards: Businesses will meet regulatory requirements while gaining competitive advantages. Using strategies proven to be effective, personal and business identities no longer are jeopardized and financial institutions no longer risk noncompliance. In short, identity theft stops here.

INTRODUCTION

Identity theft can be prevented. Contrary to common thought, most identities are stolen from businesses; fewer are stolen from garbage Dumpsters or by online hackers. Although thefts do occur from these sources (as well as from homes, cars, and persons), the majority of identity thefts are committed inside the workplace by a relatively few dishonest employees who steal the personal identification data of their coworkers and customers—a company's most valued assets. To safeguard these potential victims, and the company's interests, the workplace must be secured.

Because identity thefts occur so often in the workplace, businesses also are victims. In his keynote speech at the 2000 White Collar Crime Summit in Los Angeles, California's attorney general, William Lockyer, warned that identity theft was the greatest threat to the financial economy of businesses and the entire United States. Since then, and despite his warning, identity theft has escalated worldwide and continues unabated. The reason in great part is that no international security standards exist to protect personal information, such as the identities of U.S. citizens.

Nevertheless, federal laws now require *all* businesses to secure personal identifiers and document this or risk being fined. Nowhere, however, are businesses told *how* they might do this. Granted, each of several federal laws recommends database and computer security—but computers do not steal identities. Information technology (IT) cannot by itself secure personal information because, and perhaps to some degree due to those already secured IT systems, employee insider theft is the source of most stolen identities.

1

In the field of criminal justice, when the source of a crime is known, the incidence of that crime can be mitigated and even prevented. *Preventing Identity Theft in Your Business: How to Protect Your Business, Customers, and Employees* shows how manager-employee teams (managers have the decision power to authorize employee-designed solutions) can use step-by-step instructions in a series of consecutively ordered exercises to combat identity theft in the workplace. *Preventing Identity Theft* is written with employees in mind, to help protect them and because employees are the key to securing the workplace.

Employees are the persons closest to the workplaces and work processes where identity thefts occur. Some employees perform the job tasks required to process, update, and otherwise maintain and manage personal information contained on applications, healthcare forms, payroll and benefits checks, and other documents, both paper and digital. Those employees are positioned to recognize the work processes most susceptible to identity thefts; and those employees, therefore, also are the key individuals capable of securing those work processes.

But what exactly is an "identity"? In the evolution of crime, identity theft is a particularly fast-moving, ever-changing, and overarching crime that facilitates many ancillary identity crimes. In Part I, therefore, the first priorities are to update yesterday's definitions of identity theft and report on recent events and trends that, disturbingly, point to even greater incidence and variations in identity crimes. Included in the text is a discussion on "identity rape," the insidious effects on victims (both persons and businesses), and several sections detailing facts on why identity theft may never be completely eradicated.

The material in Part I is based on knowledge derived from reported experiences in the Identity Theft Crime and Research Lab at the Michigan State University–Business Identity Theft Partnerships in Prevention, established in 1999. As director of the lab and through work with law enforcement and businesses, and as professor of Information Security Management at the MSU School of Criminal Justice, the author has come face-to-face with the crime, the victims, and even some of the criminals. The *insider* modus operandi of identity thieves is now well known—which is why this crime can be prevented. And, from 18 years of training and applied work as an industrial-organizational (I/O) psychologist, the author has developed applied management methods to do this.

Beginning in Part II and continuing in Part III, the chapters describe a Business Information Security Program using methods from criminal justice, I/O psychology, and the management sciences. Each chapter leads the manager-employee team through workshop exercises to secure personal identifying information across four fronts: personnel, processes, proprietary information, and virtual property—the e-business Web site.

The chapter exercises to secure personnel integrate security into the traditional functions of recruitment, personnel selection, organizational socialization, and performance feedback. All personnel functions, beginning with the very basic job analysis, must be driven by sensitivity to security. The teams learn where to obtain or how to develop valid and reliable security instruments that meet the Equal Employment Opportunity Commission guidelines and Title VII statutes for fairness in personnel practices.

For some people, personnel selection, appraisal, and other practices can be threatening. In *Preventing Identity Theft in Your Business*, employees and managers take the lead in preventing identity theft in the workplace. The team designs and then oversees the personnel functions that will safeguard their security at work to protect them from the dishonest few, often temporary or contract workers. Thus, exercises in several chapters are devoted to protecting a business's most important asset and the *first front*: the people.

In succeeding chapters, the team conducts information process risk assessments to prevent the theft of personal information as it is processed through sequential job tasks, thus securing the *second front*: the work processes. The focus is on the job *position* and not the incumbent employee, because people come and go but job positions remain relatively stable. And there is no need to personalize identity theft prevention. It is a *workplace* problem.

In the concluding chapters, the team (or teams) conducts a Web Site Risk Assessment of the virtual property—the *third front*—and the team then establishes a Customer Security Program. The Web Site Risk Assessment, unlike IT security audits or assessments, measures *customer perceptions* of e-shopping security while visiting the business's online store. The Customer Security Program provides feedback and outcome measures while also helping customers protect their *future* flow of personal information, thereby avoiding victimization. Throughout, the aim is to secure the *fourth front*: proprietary, personal information.

The chapter exercises, enhanced by the management solutions they produce, are grounded in scientific theory. Based on practices from criminal justice, industrial-organizational psychology, and the management sciences, and written in easy-to-understand lay language, the chapter exercises also rely on many of the same tools businesses already use to develop "quality" standards.

This quality-to-security adaptation will be an especially easy transition for many businesses whose employees are adept at formal brainstorming, flow-charting, and other effective quality management practices. The applications and instructions for the quality-to-security management exercises and for the (perhaps) less familiar I/O psychology exercises are accompanied with illustrations of specific examples.

Identity theft is a devastating crime that undermines the economy and the very security of these United States. Its severity is not to be minimized. Legislation continues to be enacted in keeping with the continuing evolution of the crime, but legislation alone will not prevent it. To comply, therefore, with current laws as well as those that will be enacted in the future, businesses need to adopt a practical approach with specific procedures that extend the quality practices already in place and simultaneously guarantee "information" security. Once completed, these objectives can comprehensively, consistently, and over time secure a business from the threat of identity thefts.

The final product is a Business Information Security Program (BISP) that can be established with minimal costs to serve as an international security standard. Financial institutions, healthcare organizations, and *your* business can now comply with federal laws, and prove it.

PART I

THE CURRENT STATE OF IDENTITY THEFT

He that filches from me my good name robs me of
that which enriches him and makes me poor indeed.

Shakespeare, *Othello* (3.3180-86)

CHAPTER 1

WHAT IS AN "IDENTITY"?

The term "identity" is commonly used arbitrarily and imprecisely in popular media and literature, and the terms "identity theft" and "identity crime" are frequently used interchangeably. Occasional misuses or misinterpretations are not surprising because in the contemporary context, the traditional meanings underlying those concepts have become increasingly known as information and information technology (IT). Formal definitions of identity concepts are therefore in order.

IDENTITY THEFT VERSUS IDENTITY CRIME

The *Oxford English Dictionary* defines "identity" as "the set of behavioral or personal characteristics by which an individual is recognized." The traditional use of the word "identity" spoke to one's name, familial membership, and occupation (among other applications). The contemporary meaning of "identity" has, however, assumed a candidly IT connotation that extends traditional meanings to include such things as one's consumer and credit histories, financial accounts, and Social Security number. It is this contemporary usage of "identity" that is at issue when it comes to conceptualizing identity theft and identity crime.

Identity theft is a burgeoning crime of relatively recent origin. To be sure, identity theft is dynamic in nature, as it has evolved over time. As fast as new legislative definitions of identity theft have been framed and novel techniques for enforcing those definitions have emerged, identity predators have abandoned old methods in favor of new and sometimes ingeniously innovative approaches. As the crime has evolved, so also has its descriptions and definitions.

For instance, "identity theft," most commonly thought of as the theft of an individual's *personal* identifying information, has evolved to include a new twist: *business* identity theft.

Further, the theft and fraudulent use of Social Security numbers now assigned babies at birth has, most recently, led to *child* identity theft, much the same way the crime of adult pornography evolved to include those crimes on children. Also similarly, *child* identity theft is now considered a subset of a more general category of crime: *personal* identity theft. Additionally, "identity theft" is defined as a felonious crime per se, that is, as an offense in and of itself, wherein one party steals sensitive information from another, either an individual or a business entity.

Identity *theft*, however, is to be distinguished from identity *crimes*—those offenses committed using the stolen *personal* or *business* identifying information—or "identities." Thus, the conceptual relationship between identity theft and identity crime is that the former facilitates the latter. In short, stolen identities often are used to commit many other crimes, which is why identity theft also can be viewed as an all-encompassing or overarching megacrime. Legislation, investigations, and the prevention of identity theft can take different approaches, depending on the type of identity stolen. Thus, to mitigate and prevent identity thefts requires that each type of identity be clearly delineated: personal, business, and overarching.

"PERSONAL" IDENTITY THEFT

Personal identity theft is the unauthorized acquisition of another individual's personally sensitive identifying information; personal identity *crime* is the use of such information to obtain credit, goods, services, money, or property, or to commit a felony or a misdemeanor. "Personally sensitive identifying information" means a person's name, address, telephone number, driver's license number, Social Security number, place of employment, employee identification number, demand deposit account number, savings or checking account number, credit card number, or mother's maiden name—information needed to obtain an original birth certification for a complete identity takeover. With a birth certificate, mother's maiden name, and a Social Security number, for example, other governmental documents and records can be accessed; a passport and visas successfully applied for; and driver's licenses, court records, and other information fraudulently obtained and used to commit identity crimes.

Perpetrators use stolen personal identities to drain checking, savings, and retirement accounts; create bogus checks; open new credit card and bank accounts; take over existing accounts; apply for telecommunication and utility services; obtain home, automobile, college-tuition and other loans; open retail accounts; purchase airline, rail, and other transportation accommodations; rent hotel/motel rooms; rent or purchase automobiles; pay for medical supplies, prescriptions, and healthcare services; obtain employment; engage in money laundering, drug trafficking, and other organized crime; and commit acts of terror against the United States. Some, but not all, of these crimes also are committed using stolen business identities, which are to be distinguished from personal identities.

"BUSINESS" IDENTITY THEFT

Business identity theft is the unauthorized acquisition of a business's "business identifying information." Business identity *crime* is the use of such information to obtain credit, goods, services, money, or property, or to commit a felony or misdemeanor. "Business identifying information" means a business's name, address, telephone number, corporate credit card numbers, banking account numbers, federal employer identification number (FEIN), Treasury Identification Number (TIN), State Treasury Number (TN), electronic filing identification number (EFIN: Internal Revenue Service), electronic transmitter identification number

(ETIN: Internal Revenue Service), e-business Web sites, URL addresses, and e-mail addresses.

Business identity theft has become increasingly common for three reasons.

1. Corporate credit card, bank, and other account statements generally have many more entries than the accounts of average individuals and, therefore, are more complex and less easily reconciled.
2. Corporate credit card accounts usually carry higher dollar limits than do individual accounts.
3. Many employees oftentimes are authorized to use a single corporate account. In this case, the theft and fraudulent use of the account number is less easily detected in the corporate credit card statement than in an individual credit statement, which contains fewer account entries.

Alarmingly, the theft of a business's state and federal identifiers has opened the doors to new crimes of business impersonations, such as "subsidiary" fraud. This is the registration, usually with a secretary of state, of a fraudulent subsidiary company using a legitimate business's identifiers. With the payment of a modest registration fee, in some states as little as $25, parasite subsidiary "businesses" can be formed and pose as legitimate businesses, incurring never-to-be-paid expenses for goods and services and obtaining cash through fraudulent business loans and other means. Sometimes these bogus entities defraud legitimate companies by invoicing them for services never rendered or by ordering merchandise that is then sold on the black market.

The most common personal identity crimes are credit card, bank, utilities, telecommunications, and retail (e-business and onsite) fraud. By comparison, the most common forms of business identity crimes are credit card, bank, retail account, and (of most recent origin) subsidiary fraud. These lists are growing. Increasingly, other crimes and new adaptations of crimes are being committed by using stolen identities, both personal and business—which is why the theft of an identity is, in and of itself, an all-encompassing and overarching crime.

IDENTITY THEFT AS AN "OVERARCHING" CRIME

Identity theft is the crime of the twenty-first century, because identity theft is a crime overarching and enabling many other types of crime. For example, stolen identities are used to commit credit card and bank fraud; retail account, utilities, and telecommunications fraud; mortgage and loan fraud; employment fraud; mail fraud; wire fraud; drug trafficking; money laundering; government documents and benefits fraud; prize, sweepstakes, and lottery scams; Internet auction fraud; online stalking and harassment; pornography distribution and consumption; human smuggling (women, children, and illegal immigrants); e-business fraud and a host of other cybercrimes; and terrorism.

According to federal authorities, identity theft is a key catalyst in funding terrorism.[1] Most, if not all, acts of terror against the United States are thought to have been accomplished by the use of fake or stolen identities, including the bombings of the U.S. embassies in Kenya and Tanzania, of the USS *Cole*, of the Marine Corps barracks in Lebanon, of the World Trade Center in 1993, and the atrocities of September 11, 2001. The al Qaeda training manual describes "key missions" that consist of "blasting and destroying" places of amusement, bridges into and out of cities, and embassies.[2] Not mentioned is the conversion of commercial airlines into homicidal guided missiles, although we now know that terrorists also financed these and other attacks using authentic (i.e., stolen versus fabricated) identities, impersonating real people with actual birth and credit records.

In fact, when leaving their training camps in Afghanistan or elsewhere, the "brothers" are provided five discrete sets of identities and given explicit instructions on how and when to use them. For example, when using the identity of a given individual, the impersonator is to speak the language of that individual and dress according to the custom of the individual's identity. Lesson 3 in the al Qaeda manual gives these instructions:

> The brother who has special work status (commander, communication link...) should have more than one identity card and passport. He should learn the contents of each, the nature of the

(indicated) profession, and the dialect of the residence area listed in
the document (p. 22).

In one reported case of identity theft, tens of thousands of foreigners
illegally obtained Social Security numbers (SSNs) from the U.S. Social
Security Administration.[3] Such an action raises cause for great concern:
Once terrorists secure stolen names, addresses, Social Security numbers,
and other personal identifiers, they frequently use these identifiers to
create bogus passports and driver's licenses, to open bank accounts, to
rent automobiles, and to otherwise cover up their nefarious activities.
Extremist groups target American businesses and institutions because of
the severe financial impact their terrorist acts inflict. Identity theft,
therefore, is an overarching crime that enables many other crimes, including terrorism and the devastation it wreaks.

There are no national security standards in place to prevent identity
thefts and the resulting wave of identity crimes. Independent businesses
are ruined, and, in the aggregate, the financial infrastructure and the
very security of our nation are undermined. As will be shown, the effects
on people and businesses already have been devastating.

CHAPTER 2

IDENTITY THEFT: EFFECTS ON VICTIMS

The victims of identity theft and identity crime, respectively, are the individuals and businesses whose identities have been stolen and the individuals and businesses who are defrauded using such stolen identities. The "theft" and the "crime" are two different offenses, each with its own structure of penalties and fines. Also to be distinguished are the effects of these crimes on persons versus businesses. Both suffer the financial losses, but for persons there also is an emotional component that sometimes is so intense that even the term "identity rape" is inadequately descriptive.

EFFECTS ON PERSONS

People may be made aware that they are victims of identity theft in a number of ways, including when they:

- Receive a telephone call from the diligent fraud department of a bank, credit union, or other financial institution, inquiring about a recent credit application
- Are contacted by a collections department or agency asking why their account is delinquent
- Discover unauthorized long-distance calls on their telephone or cell phone bill
- Discover fraudulent checks deducted on their checking account statements

- Are notified by a bank or credit union of an overdrawn account or dishonored checks
- Are contacted by a merchant or other business demanding payment for nonsufficient funds (NSF) charges and returned checks
- Discover unauthorized withdrawals on their checking, savings, or investment account statements
- Are unexpectedly denied credit, such as for a mortgage, auto loan, credit card or retail account
- Are arrested for a crime they did not commit

Experiences from working with victims of identity theft since 1999 at the Michigan State University (MSU) Identity Theft Crime and Research Lab reveal some interesting findings on the effects of identity crimes. First, even when the financial loss is minimal, many victims suffer emotionally as much or even more than do victims of other types of crimes. The term "identity rape" describes the personal violation experienced by many victims after learning that someone is using their name, personal identification numbers, and other information usually known only by the victim or maintained on supposedly private financial records. Many victims have described the thought that someone, somewhere, perhaps at this very moment, is posing as them as an abusive violation and fear-filled invasion of one's most intimate, private self. The financial impact, although also stressful, often is secondary to the initial emotional distress experienced by victims and the open-ended fear that they and family members may be victimized again and are vulnerable to the predations of the sleeper criminal.

A pervasive observation noted from working with identity theft victims is that, regardless of gender, age, or race, the psychological effects are experienced as a continuum of emotions similar to those suffered by victims of other forms of abuse.

Continuum of Psychological Effects

When victims learn of the identity theft, they have no way of knowing the extent of their potential financial losses and other consequences.

They are aware only that some criminal, somewhere, has assumed their person and their resources. The initial response is *shock*: "This can't be happening to me; it only happens to others" is a commonly reported sentiment. Some victims *fear* that the criminal may cause physical harm, as well, either to them or to a family member, and many victims *panic* when they realize the potential scope of financial losses and the range of possible future consequences caused by the unknown predator. Initially, the victims do not know how many or which bank accounts—checking, savings, retirement—have been accessed or the amount of the financial loss, or how many and what kinds of credit cards have been obtained, retail accounts opened, or other fraudulent transactions that may be under way or already completed.

These uncertainties, together with the realization that little or no recourse is available for the recovery of the financial losses, evoke in victims a sense of *helplessness* over their situations and a *lack of control* over how to stop or further prevent the crime. Without exception, victims soon become *frustrated* when they attempt to file fraud alerts with the credit reporting agencies and are able to reach only an automated machine or, worse yet, when they are able to reach a customer service agent, they find that employee to be negative, insensitive, and sometimes even argumentative, perhaps due to the employee's own frustrations from dealing with overburdened identity caseloads. And frustration unresolved turns to *depression* and *anger*.

The intensity and gravity of these psychological effects on victims depends on the individuals' personalities as well as on the relative amount of financial losses and other specifics of their personal situations. For example, in the case of a recently retired couple whose retirement savings had been wiped out, the husband became severely clinically depressed, and the wife, through a power of attorney authorization, was left to deal with the myriad consequences of the theft.

In another example, a single mother working to support herself and her young child was arrested on a warrant for a traffic citation she did not receive. Upon appearing in court to contest the charge, the victim was nonetheless fined and lost her driver's license. When two subsequent warrants were served for other crimes she also did not commit, the victim lost her job and was about to be evicted from her apartment. Working with the chief judge of the district, the secretary of state, and other government officials, the MSU Identity Theft Crime Lab victim advocates helped clear the victim of the fraudulent charges. Doing so, however, consumed over 100 hours of time and cost the victim an estimated $5,000 in out-of-pocket expenses in addition to her emotional duress. (Note, however, neither the Michigan State University-Business Partnerships in Prevention nor the ID Theft Crime and Research Lab—outreach initiatives established in 1999 by the author—charges victims for assisting them.)

These examples are only two of many that serve to illustrate the range and depth of emotions experienced by some victims, whose problems can go on indefinitely.

Reconciling and clearing credit histories and accounts where fraudulent charges have been made are time-consuming activities that can take days, weeks, or months; sometimes the situation is insoluble. For some victims, the resulting frustration leads to anger and despair as they repeatedly must prove to credit agencies and businesses that they are not the offender.

Over time, most victims reach a point of acceptance—that a crime has been committed; it could happen again even though preventive measures have been taken to protect the future flow of personal information. The feelings of *acceptance* come, however, only in the last stage of a sometimes difficult and lengthy process of recovery. The continuum of emotions, ranging from shock to panic, fear, helplessness, and lack of control, even depression and anger, and to eventually acceptance, cannot be traversed overnight.

Experience working with executives from a major U.S. automaker whose identities were stolen by a contract worker on her last day of work revealed that people whose job tasks involve day-to-day problem solving and trouble-shooting recover sooner than do some others, such as those whose job tasks or daily life experiences are relatively more routine.[1] These executives, perhaps because of their problem-solving

skills and experiences, were able to quickly clear credit records and resolve related problems. They did not suffer the emotional consequences
as intensively as do many other victims. Nonetheless, regardless of person, personality, or position, the recovery *process*, unlike the specific experience of victimization, is the same for all victims.

The process of healing begins when victims become involved in doing
whatever they can do themselves to control their own situations. Victims' feelings of helplessness are replaced with feelings of control once
they first report the crime to the police, then go through the sometimes
many steps to file fraud alerts with each of the credit reporting
agencies—Experian, Equifax, and TransUnion—work with retail accounts and other businesses to clear credit records, place passwords on
banking and other financial institution accounts, and take other precautions to prevent further victimization.

A victim's personal involvement is a positive step and important factor that serves as a catharsis for recovery through the emotionally
charged stages of shock, panic, fear, helplessness, frustration, and anger
to, finally, acceptance. Unfortunately, accepting that a crime has been
committed does not mean that all effects of the crime have been resolved.

Other Effects on Victims

In addition to the continuum of common emotions, victims of identity
theft and identity crime also suffer from other short- and long-term
effects, such as the *loss of productivity* at work and at home. Time usually spent at work or with families and friends and on routine activities
is now consumed with telephone calls, letters to creditors, and personal
meetings to clear fraudulent accounts or criminal records. Depending on
the complexity of the crime—the length of time the stolen identity was
used, the number of identity crimes that were committed, and the number of states or countries involved in the identity network—the lost productivity at work and home and the time to recovery can be hours,
weeks, or even months.

Further, even before reports that most identities are stolen in the workplace,[2] victims seen at the MSU Identity Theft Crime Lab reported *distrust* of coworkers whom they suspected of being the predators. This distrust reportedly extends to various degrees of *paranoia* and even isolation from others at work—not very conducive for high job performance or for a healthy work environment.

At home, victims go to greater or lesser extents to restore and protect their privacy. Some measures are removing names from telephone directories and screening phone calls, sometimes after installing expensive but sophisticated technology; canceling credit cards and retail accounts, thereafter using only cash; and closing accounts and changing banks. One victim dropped her first name altogether and went to the time and trouble of replacing her first name with her middle name on all personal and work documents and records.

Victims frequently report *strained relationships* with spouses and family members due to the concentrated focus of attention on the financial problems resulting from the identity thefts, the unrelenting stress due to the disruptions at work, and the difficulties encountered in trying to resolve the identity crimes. There are, therefore, many consequences for victims of identity theft, and most victims suffer them all to one degree or another.

Resolving Normalcy

In most cases, the criminals are not caught, and, contrary to advertisements by some companies trying to sell prevention, stolen identities cannot be "found," "reclaimed," or "recovered." Victims, nonetheless, move through the emotional stages toward recovery as they protect themselves from possible future losses by placing passwords on bank, credit card, and retail accounts; taking precautions at restaurants, gas stations, and wherever they use credit cards; limiting or discontinuing debit card transactions; doing business with financial institutions, retail stores, and others that are known for having taken identity theft precautions; and otherwise securing their personal identifying information (see Chapter 20). Sooner or later, victims gain a sense of acceptance of their situations and are able to resume their normal home and work lives.

Some Victims Are Revictimized

Once stolen, a Social Security number, name, address, or other form of identity may be fraudulently used again and again. The first time around, criminals use the stolen identities to commit "primary" fraud—the fraudulent purchase of goods and services. Later on, after the victim has placed fraud alerts on credit reports to help prevent further fraudulent financial transactions, criminals use the stolen identities to commit "secondary" fraud.

In secondary fraud, criminals use the victim's identifying information on credit cards, driver's licenses, and other documents they falsely create and use only for "secondary" purposes of identification, such as to rent public or private post office boxes for the delivery of merchandise fraudulently ordered over the phone or on the Internet. Public and private post offices rarely if ever check the credit reporting agencies for credit histories of postal patrons.

Within the context of secondary fraud, identity crime is rarely a one-person offense. That is, the use of the one victim's identity as secondary fraud typically occurs when a member of the crime network rents the post office box to receive fraudulent merchandise, which is purchased by another network member using yet a second victim's stolen identity. In this case, there are (at least) two criminals and two victims—the primary victim and the secondary, unknowingly revictimized, victim. The technique by which each of several criminals is responsible for a different task in the chain of a crime is called "layering." The trail of the crime is more difficult to trace, no one criminal is responsible for the entire crime yet all share in the rewards, and as accomplices, each criminal is beholden to all others.

In one case seen at the MSU Identity Theft Crime Lab, a victim in 1999 became and remained a secondary victim until at least 2001, when the U.S. Secret Service assumed the investigation. The "secondary" offense was discovered in an investigation of an identity theft case where a MasterCard was used as identification to open a post office box in California. The name on the MasterCard was traced to an individual in Illinois who, upon further investigation, was discovered to have been a "primary" victim of bank identity theft in 1999, when living in the East Coast. Secondary identity fraud, though common, is only one form of revictimization.

A common and perhaps more egregious form is the revictimization of a victim by unscrupulous businesses that capitalize on the psychological sufferings of identity theft victims. Many victims and nonvictims alike subject themselves to the pressures of identity theft by purchasing solutions for prevention from increasing numbers of insurance companies, prepaid legal services, Web site "help" desks that provide victim advocacy for a fee, and even financial institutions that charge their own customers for help. Susceptible victims and nonvictims alike fall prey to "protection-for-pay" plans they should not need. Unfortunately, today a growing number of businesses are seeking to capitalize on the emotions evoked by the threat of identity theft.

Victims Need Not Pay

Victims do not need to pay for help or protection. Today there exists any number of freely available sources of assistance for victims of identity theft and identity crime. Police departments are becoming increasingly more involved in identity crimes and in advising victims of the necessary steps they must take for protection. There also are many nonprofit agencies or programs staffed by trained professionals who specialize in identity theft and identity crime victim advocacy. The Identity Theft Resource Center in San Diego is one such program; another is the MSU Identity Theft Crime and Research Lab.[3] Both the Resource Center and the Research Lab, affiliated only by their common interest in identity theft advocacy and prevention, have Web sites that provide step-by-step instructions to help victims of identity theft, and one-on-one counseling is available online or in person. Some banks and credit card companies now also provide, without charge, identity theft and crime assistance for their customers. Many independent businesses also attempt to help customers who have been victimized, and many businesses also become victims and suffer the effects of identity theft.

At least one federal agency, the Federal Trade Commission (FTC), has a Web site that provides identity theft victims with detailed instructions, and victims may report their crime to that agency by completing an online complaint form.[4] The FTC does not investigate the crime, but the information that victims volunteer is used to track identity crime trends and practices, for purposes of prediction and prevention. The FTC also will mail anyone a manual with instructions on whom and where to contact in an effort to prevent further, or any, identity abuse.

EFFECTS ON BUSINESSES

Businesses suffer in at least three ways from identity theft.

1. Financial institutions, retail businesses, and service providers bear the burden of the costs for fraudulently purchased merchandise or services using the stolen identity of an employee, customer, or patient.
2. A business's own identity may be used to fraudulently purchase merchandise or services from other business entities.
3. Criminals fraudulently use business identities as their modus operandi for obtaining the identities of people, such as when criminals clone and then use a business Web site to collect personal identities from the legitimate business's customers—a scheme known as phishing.

Examples of Business Identity Theft

An example of phishing is the case in which the International Chamber of Commerce uncovered a global Internet banking scam involving about $3.9 billion.[5] The identity thieves had set up fake Web sites that were identical to the sites of original businesses. By mimicking legitimate banking businesses, the criminals obtained customer Social Security numbers and bank and credit account numbers. The *motive* was to obtain cash, and the modus operandus, or method, was the phishing scam.

Identity theft criminals also impersonate a business when using its name to *telephone* customers under the auspices of updating accounts or verifying account information, with the underlying motive of obtaining the customers' SSNs, credit card, bank, or other identifiers.[6] This example is an adaptation of phishing (by telephone) whereby the criminal impersonates the business so as to impersonate an individual.

The "business identity" also may be a company's credit card account number, bank account number, payroll information on employees, and one or more federal or state tax numbers. The business identity also can be passwords and access codes for buildings, offices, and departments where financial records are maintained and for computers and computer server systems.

At a major U. S. automaker, for example, employees or individuals impersonating employees used the company's pass code—considered proprietary, identifying information—to gain access to Experian Credit Agency credit reports on as many as 13,000 consumers.[7] Credit reports contain names, SSNs, birth dates, account numbers for American Express, Visa, Discover, and other credit cards, department store credit account numbers, bank names and account numbers, and numerous other pieces of personal information that can be, and are, used to commit crimes of fraud and facilitate acts of terror.

Another large-scale business identity theft occurred at a national computer company where identity thieves stole a company laptop to access names and Social Security numbers of over 700 employees.[8] In another reported case, three Florida men used stolen personal identities to obtain temporary employment at several businesses for the purpose of stealing business identities—the businesses' banking account numbers, which they then used to create and print counterfeit checks. By the time the crimes were detected, the men had fraudulently purchased more than $250,000 in merchandise using the bogus business checks. In a separate but similar case, inside criminals obtained and used corporate payroll information to create and cash bogus payroll checks. Additionally, in Fisher's Landing, Washington, perpetrators broke into the mailbox of a real estate company to steal outgoing checks, which they then reproduced.[9] This theft is one form of mail fraud used increasingly to obtain both individual and business identities. Unsecured residential and business mailboxes are easy "picks." Criminals case the neighborhoods and business locations, know who is and who is not at home or at work and the time the mail is delivered, and simply retrieve a victim's mail containing SSNs, bank information, and other identifiers. One minute on a computer from any location turns such identity thefts into identity crimes when the criminal accesses a business (or personal) bank account or makes fraudulent online purchases of merchandise.

Thus, in these and other ways, criminals use stolen business identities to access a business's financial accounts and employee records and to create bogus checks, open new credit card and bank accounts, take over existing accounts, and gain access to offices and even homes of employees and customers. The effects on businesses are enormous.

Other Effects on Businesses

The financial losses for business identity theft are the costs due to the loss of merchandise from the thefts and other financial losses from the thefts and fraudulent use of business credit card and bank account numbers. Additional costs to businesses are the losses accrued when customers who, on learning their identities have been stolen, cancel their accounts and move to other financial institutions, discontinue current credit card accounts, and stop shopping at their usual retail or other stores—all without considering that no business is immune, and that the business, too, is a victim.

Costs too difficult to measure include employee time that must be allocated to resolving the issues of a business identity theft; the costs for auditors to review accounting and operating procedures; the employee time involvement with customers of the business whose accounts have been accessed; and the loss of productivity on the "other" jobs the employees were principally hired to perform. Also difficult to assess precisely are employee costs associated with decreased job satisfaction, pay satisfaction, and other costs attributable to work-overload stress and (when applicable) concomitant healthcare costs that occur as a result of work problems manifesting themselves either physically and/or emotionally.

Additionally, a potentially devastating cost to business victims of identity theft and/or identity crime is negative word-of-mouth advertising originating from the victimized customer who perceives having been offered little, if any, assistance from the business itself or, worse yet, who finds fault with the business for failing to provide adequate identification security.

Although routinely reported in the media as "estimates," the costs of identity theft to business are largely impossible to gauge precisely, not only for each of the reasons above but also because the crime of identity *theft* is the precursor to identity *crime*. That is to say, for example, an estimate for the costs of credit card fraud likely involves one and usually more offenses, such as retail account fraud, telecommunications and utilities fraud, and, increasingly, organized crime and drug trafficking. The financial effects of identity theft on businesses, therefore, are largely unknown.

Despite not knowing the costs of even one identity theft and identity crime, and given reasons why reported costs are in effect gross *under*estimates, it is certain that identity thefts and identity crimes negatively impact managers, employees, the work environment, and levels of work output. It is, therefore, reasonable to assert that identity theft unchecked will upset the economic equilibrium of the entire Untied States and beyond. It is frightening to recognize, as the next chapter discloses, that identity theft and identity crimes are entrenched in our society and that they are here to stay.

CHAPTER 3

IDENTITY CRIME
IS ENTRENCHED

The need for business standards of information security has never been greater. In the United States, "information technology" and "database management" are characteristic themes of the information era. To this list might be added "identity marketing." We are a nation of databases that aggregate, consolidate, and disseminate worldwide the names, addresses, Social Security numbers (SSNs), and other personal information of U.S. citizens. From the time of birth, when newborns are assigned SSNs, and forever after, even beyond death, every citizen becomes a number in one or more databases. Many people may share the same name—first, middle, and last—but no two share the same nine-digit database identifier. Identity crime is entrenched in our society and is here to stay. Why? Because identity crimes are low-risk offenses with high payoffs, and the SSNs with which the criminals work are easily accessible. Most every business today has at least one database complete with these numbers.

Small and large businesses alike use a wide range of computerized systems to efficiently manage, control, and maintain information on products purchased and sold, services bought and rendered, salaries and healthcare benefits earned and paid, and other business activities that use the SSNs of employees and customers. For many businesses, SSNs are financial commodities bought and sold on the market. Many companies, for example, purchase identities, often with the option to resell them

25

later. These sales of personal information for marketing purposes are examples of how identities become a part of many databases without the knowledge or permission of the person whose information is sold.

This "identity marketing" also explains why "opting out" of direct marketing lists—the request to remove a name from marketing lists—is only temporary; the purchaser of the marketing list also may purchase the option to sell the identities to third parties who, in turn, may resell the list to others, and so on. Identity thieves do this on the street; that is, criminals sell lists of identities to one another. On the street, of course, this practice of selling identities is a crime.

Identity marketing places a great many individuals at risk because, given that many of the database systems in use are unsecured in the first place, the more times a person's identity is marketed, the greater the likelihood that someone, somewhere will steal that identity and use it for underhanded purposes. It is simply a matter of probability, with increasing chances as new identity databases continue to be developed and disseminated. One recent example is the most comprehensive database in terms of the numbers of people tracked and the types of personal information stored, the database overseen by the Health Insurance Portability and Accountability Act.[1]

HIPAA DATABASE

Anyone who recently has visited a doctor's office or other medical facility has been asked to sign a form acknowledging receipt of information outlining rights under the Health Insurance Portability and Accountability Act, or HIPAA. Meant to ease information sharing between medical professionals and billing to third-party payers, HIPAA oversees a national database containing personal information on everyone with healthcare coverage or who have in the past received health services. HIPAA, which became official and legally effective for all healthcare-related organizations in October 2003, unwittingly opened a new avenue for increasing numbers of potential identity thefts.

The HIPAA database contains names, addresses, SSNs, physical and psychological details, and other data on individuals and their family members. According to the act, healthcare-related institutions can disclose this information to any number of other organizations and individuals for purposes directly *and indirectly* related to treatment, payment, healthcare operations, benefits, and services. Therefore, this sensitive information is accessible by all healthcare institutions, such as hospitals, clinics, pharmacies, private practitioners, and medical supply houses, as well as by second- and third-party clearinghouses including database management companies, suppliers, and vendors. In other words, thousands of institutions and hundreds of thousands of their employees now have access to the personal information on millions of U.S. citizens. Yet, except for computer system security, no security standards are required for institutions that have access to this mammoth HIPAA database.

The Health Insurance Portability and Accountability Act and its provisions are essential for the maintenance of the healthcare system and, thus, valuable to many U.S. citizens. The database provides for the efficient transmission of information and payments between healthcare insurers and providers, and the act contains features beneficial to employees, disabled persons, and seniors. Yet this unsecured national identity database exposes these same persons to risk for abuse by identity theft criminals. The HIPAA database, although widely accessible, is not known to be used to market identities, as some other databases are.

CREDIT AGENCY DATABASES

Three credit agencies—TransUnion, Equifax, and Experian—each keep records of the names, addresses, SSNs, and financial dealings on the majority of U.S. citizens. These agencies sell personal information to other businesses that pay to verify a customer's creditworthiness before completing a financial transaction, which the customer authorizes when requesting on-credit purchases. At least three of these agencies also sell information the consumer does *not* explicitly authorize, usually personal information contained in the "header" of the credit report.

The header is the first of three sections of a credit report that lists a person's primary identifiers—name, addresses, SSN, birth date, and other information. A second section contains detailed information collected over a period of years on the person's financial activities, such as the names of banks, credit card companies, mortgage and insurance companies, retail and other entities the individual has conducted business with, and the amounts of money borrowed and owed.

In the third section, the credit report lists all companies that have purchased a person's credit report, even though that person has never applied to that company for credit. Businesses use these *unauthorized* credit reports to market products and services; for example, credit card companies buy lists of information on creditworthy consumers prior to mailing them preapproved credit applications. This is one example of how identities become disseminated among databases, usually without the knowledge of the person whose identity was sold. As mentioned earlier, this also explains why the opting out of direct mailing lists is only temporary—the opted-out mailing list already has been sold to some other company, which now must also be mailed an opt-out letter. The problem is that the new company may be unknown—consumers have no control over where their identities are marketed or to whom.

Presumably, any employee of any authorized or unauthorized business that has a membership with the credit agency can access the credit agency's database. Thousands of businesses have pass codes to the credit agency databases, providing access to millions of employees worldwide. Unfortunately, credit agencies and other businesses are not required to request consumers' permissions to market identities, nor are consumers informed of, or compensated for, the sale of their identities. Ironically, indeed, people requesting their own, personal credit information often must pay for it.

Credit reporting agencies are critical to the financial success of businesses and the economic infrastructure of the United States. Businesses must be able to legitimately determine the creditworthiness of individuals who seek to obtain products or services based on their abilities to pay. However, credit agencies, and the business customers these agencies sell information to, operate on the edge of illegitimacy when they sell citizens' identities without first having invested in an information security program that would protect those citizens' personal identifiers. Although the numbers of available and accessible databases may border on the infinite, another stark example will serve to illuminate the burgeoning identity crisis.

GOVERNMENT DATABASES

The U.S. government maintains many unsecured databases on private citizens. Perhaps the most comprehensive after HIPAA (because they do not contain the physical and psychological histories) are those databases maintained by the Social Security Administration and the U.S. Internal Revenue Service. Additionally, the U.S. Selective Service maintains an identity database on U.S. males. There are also all the drivers' license databases. Most recently, a travelers' database proposed by the Department of Homeland Security monitors individuals coming into, departing from, and traveling within the United States.

These and a variety of other governmental U.S. databases provide for efficiencies in economies, services, and homeland security; they are a benefit to U.S. citizens and essential to the government and security of the United States. Unwittingly, these and all other databases also are gold mines for identity theft and terrorist networks to facilitate financial frauds and acts of terror. Information technology (IT) alone cannot contain the threats to thefts of identities from these databases; as previously noted, computers do not steal identities. In fact, computer and network security provide only a *third* layer of protection.

The first layer of protection, and the primary source of security, concerns people—the employees who help maintain the confidentiality of personal information and who help prevent the theft of identities by the dishonest few insiders who have access to the computers and can use the databases to steal the identities of their coworkers and customers. Computerized data, however, whether downloaded or hand-copied, are only one source of the identity thefts because most jobs also process personal information in paper form—applications, certificates, receipts, accounting statements, and various other types of documents. The second layer of protection, therefore, consists of methods that can secure these *work processes*. People and work process security, together with the third layer of protection—IT security—comprise the foundation of an information security program that would secure any business, regardless of type or size, from the threat of identity theft. More than ever before, information standards for security are now needed—particularly because recent disturbing events point to escalations in identity thefts and identity crimes.

CHAPTER 4

IDENTITY CRIMES
ARE ESCALATING

Identity theft in the United States is not only entrenched, it is escalating. Identities of untold numbers of U.S. citizens are being exported to India, China, Japan, Russia, Canada, the Philippines, and elsewhere. Prosecutions of identity crimes are rare because of jurisdictional obstacles. Local law enforcement has been stripped of resources to combat identity crimes. There is little, if any, preemptive identity theft legislation, and businesses require no security standards to protect personal identities. For these reasons, identity thefts and identity crimes are predicted to increase exponentially.

OUTSOURCING IDENTITIES

Consider, first, outsourcing. Hundreds of U.S. companies seek to remain competitive by sending white-collar jobs abroad to be performed by a cheaper workforce. The types of jobs being outsourced include employee benefits, customer service centers, database management, employee payroll, and income tax preparation, to name a few. Even the credit agencies, each of which maintains databases on over 200 million U.S. consumers, outsource jobs that process credit disputes—presumably, many or even most arising from identity thefts. These and other white-collar jobs would not exist but for Social Security numbers, credit card numbers, bank account numbers, and other personal identifiers. Without this personal information, there would be no job tasks to perform and no jobs to outsource. The real truth is that it is "identities" that are being outsourced.

U.S. identities are particularly vulnerable to theft in outsourced companies because of the relatively lucrative socioeconomic statuses of many U.S. citizens, coupled with the unorthodox business practices in some outsource-target countries. Pioneering research at the Michigan State University (MSU) Identity Theft Crime and Research Lab, since corroborated in other, independently conducted, studies, indicates that, contrary to conventional understanding, approximately 50 percent or more of identity thefts in the United States are stolen from within companies rather than from "Dumpster diving," or from stolen purses or wallets, or by online hacking of computer systems.[1] An insider who steals identities may be a part-time, full-time, temporary, or permanent employee, or even an impersonator of an employee—that is, someone who hires into a company specifically to steal identities. Given that a major source of identity theft in the United States is committed by thieves inside the workplace, insider theft can reasonably be assumed to be greater in other countries, particularly countries where bribery and payoffs are known to be common business practices.

Additionally, outsourcing identities to other countries gives foreigners easy access to personal information. Thus, terrorists have more readily available sources of this personal information. Terrorists who use stolen identities to travel incognito and to conceal their terrorist activities now have U.S. identities shipped to their own backyard.

Once databases are disseminated abroad beyond U.S. boundaries, the United States has no control over the databases themselves, the identities in the databases, or investigations and prosecutions of identity crimes. Even within the United States, jurisdictional boundaries can present problems for prosecutions, should a criminal to be apprehended; these obstacles form another reason why identity crimes are escalating.

JURISDICTIONAL PROBLEMS

Identity crimes are predicted to increase because of identity outsourcing and also because identity crimes are complex and difficult both to investigate and to prosecute across legal jurisdictions. For instance, identity crimes are rarely unijurisdictional offenses. Most often, identity crimes are committed by organized networks that consist of several cells located across counties, states, and, increasingly, different countries. In the United States, a crime is prosecuted in the jurisdiction where it was committed. But with the identity *theft*, the jurisdictional location—the site of the theft—usually is unknown, which is why identity theft investigations begin at the post office drop or empty apartment where the fraudulent merchandise is delivered, and not the location where the identity was stolen, and why investigations of identity *crimes* usually lead to several, and not just one, legal jurisdiction, as illustrated in the next example from an actual case.

Perpetrators using a list of stolen identities completed numerous fraudulent credit card applications with several credit companies located in cities in several states.[2] The credit card applications were made online, over the phone, and also in person. For each application, the criminals replaced the victim's "present" legitimate address with a new, also actual, mail box address, where the credit cards were mailed to the criminal impersonators. In addition to the changed "present" address, the criminals completed sections on the applications requiring the names and addresses of the place of employment and the names and addresses of references who would attest to the credibility of the (criminal) applicant. Although the business and reference names were bogus, most of the addresses were real (and did lead to other information). The names and addresses given by the impersonating criminal—new present address, place of employment, and references—were all in one state but in different, bordering counties (i.e., in different jurisdictions). Once the criminals received the credit cards at the privately owned post office box, they used the cards to purchase merchandise online, over the phone, and in person at various retail stores; the purchases were made in different counties, cities, and states.

In this case, were the criminals to be apprehended, the question is: In which U.S. jurisdiction would these crimes be prosecuted? Usually, credit card frauds committed by organized networks are the domain of the U.S. Secret Service. This case, had it been resolved, could have been prosecuted at the federal level of jurisdiction. However, the *investigation* of this case, to bring it to prosecution, was hampered by the jurisdictional complexities.

Some jurisdictional problems are international, as in the case of the robbery of the apartment a young man in Oakland, California, in which the perpetrator(s) stole a passport, Social Security card, and other personal documents.[3] Some six months later, the man received a letter from a London bank approving a loan for the (fraudulent) purchase of a condominium. In another international case, this one involving "business" identity theft, the corporate credit card number of an Okemos, Michigan, business was stolen and used fraudulently to purchase merchandise that was traced by the MSU Crime Lab to an apartment in Romania.[4] In both of these cases, international obstacles hindered the investigations, but even if the perpetrators had been identified and apprehended, prosecutions across international jurisdictions are particularly difficult. Another, related jurisdictional problem is that identity crimes rarely are one-person offenses.

Identity networks grow rapidly to include relatives, friends, and friends of friends. Identity networks attract criminals because they know the chances for apprehension are slim, the networks are difficult to track, and payoffs are high. To illustrate the evolution of one such network, on her last day of work at a major U.S. automobile manufacturing company, a contract employee stole a list of coworker identities, then gave and sold sections of the list to others, who in turn sold sections of those lists to still others, and so on. Within six weeks, when this case was uncovered by a police task force, the network had evolved from the one contract employee to include 45 others who were directly and indirectly involved in credit card fraud, bank fraud, retail fraud, and telecommunications fraud. This crime *was* solved, but, in most cases, even with the apprehension and confession of one person in the network, chances are that a criminal may know only the immediately previous source of the stolen identity—the friend or relative from whom the identity was purchased; thus, the prosecution and conviction of these two perpetrators would not ensure curtailment of the network's continuing evolution and operation. (In fact, in this case, one cell member tracked to Philadelphia was never found.)

Yet another jurisdictional issue—the "layering" of identity crimes—points to why these crimes go unprosecuted and therefore continue. Identity crimes are "layered" so that different cells operate in different legal jurisdictions and each cell performs different but interrelated job tasks—much like some organizations departmentalize operations. In one such network, one cell used the stolen identities to create false checks; another cell's responsibility was to cash the checks; another cell manufactured secondary identities, which were used by yet another cell to open post office drops for the delivery of fraudulent merchandise purchased by yet other cells. Many of these cells operated in different jurisdictions, so the chain of criminal activities occurred across different and distinct legal boundaries.

This layering illustrates both the complexity of these offenses due to the network (cell) configurations and the jurisdictional problems encountered in these investigations, which is another reason why most identity crimes go unresolved and are predicted to increase.

POLICE LACK RESOURCES

Another reason for increases in identity thefts and concomitant crimes is because investigations are particularly costly and local law enforcement has been stripped of crime-fighting resources. Primary responsibility for fighting identity theft lies with local law enforcement, but with the establishment of the Department of Homeland Security, the federal government has reallocated resources from local agencies to the Federal Bureau of Investigation (FBI) to fight terrorism. Because of these federal cuts and also because of state funding cuts, police departments nationwide are being forced to pare budgets; freeze hiring; scale back on overtime; cutback on materials and equipment; and reduce officer training. (Some departments have been eliminated altogether.) In these circumstances, police departments are unable to give enough attention to costly investigations of identity theft.

Identity theft investigations require backtracking from the end of the crime, where the merchandise was delivered, to the primary crime scene, where the identity was stolen. Tracking an identity crime chain is costly when using traditional methods of investigation that must traverse complex network configurations with cells that sometimes operate internationally. Although advanced technology does exist to track identity crimes and criminals online, few police departments have resources for the technology or for officer training to use it. This fact is most unfortunate because online investigations are speedy, efficient, and economical—and there are no jurisdictional boundaries in cyberspace. However, the lack of funding curtails or precludes many investigations. Identity crimes will naturally, therefore, persist. Ironically, funds have been diverted to federal agencies to fight terrorism, but local law enforcement is responsible for fighting the fundamental crime that facilitates terrorism—the overarching crime of identity theft.

Legislation could mitigate and help de-escalate identity crimes. For example, resources could be reallocated or shared; jurisdictional boundaries could be redefined for collaborative cross-jurisdictional investigations and prosecutions; and, of course, security standards could be required for businesses that house identities. But so far, this is not happening.

LEGISLATION IS LACKING

As identity crime legislation continues to be proposed and enacted, identity crimes are on the increase and criminals continue to discover new modus operandi to, in effect, stay ahead of the law. The misappropriation of "business" identities is a developing extension of traditional "personal" identity theft, with variations such as subsidiary theft and also, recently, phishing—the cloning of a legitimate business Web site to obtain customer identities. Although criminals will continue to develop novel methods to commit identity crimes, effective legislation, were it to be enacted, can thwart their attempts.

Granted, some legislation—the Gramm-Leach-Bliley Act, the Federal Trade Commission Privacy Rule, the Safeguard Rule, and others—*does* require information technology (IT) security compliance to help mitigate and prevent computer and network system breaches, such as hacking and phishing.[5] However, IT security does not also secure people and processes and also will not safeguard personal information, absent other security measures.

If it existed, legislation involving people and process security would be preemptive, as are the IT security laws. Unfortunately, however, most current laws are neither proactive nor preventive; the laws are, rather, reactive and hastily enacted, and many reflect a lack of knowledge about the crime, the criminal, and the victim. Not surprisingly, many "experts" who testify at legislative hearings exhibit only peripheral visions of identity theft causes and consequences. There are understandable reasons why this is true. For one, until late 2003, most police departments refused to take identity theft complaints—some still do not—and those that do, often file away the complaints, never to act on them, all because of the jurisdictional problems and costs of investigating these complaints. In short, even though they have been slow to focus attention on identity crimes, law enforcement officials are the presumed experts on crime and thus most often sought after to give testimony at identity theft legislative hearings. Unfortunately, those not close to the crime cannot know it very well and cannot, therefore, expertly inform legislative decision making.

In addition to law enforcement, victim "experts" also are called to testify in legislative hearings. However, the knowledge that victims' testimony provides is anecdotal: Their vision and understanding of what has occurred is often blurred from the duress of the offenses; and their testimonies, charged with subjectivity and emotion, can be superficial and misleading. The quality of legislative information, therefore, is often insufficient as a basis for enacting laws to prevent identity theft and identity crimes. Doubtless, this is why most legislation is merely reactive and not preventive.

Current reactive laws increase penalties and fines, although volumes of criminal justice research show punishment fails to deter. Nonetheless, if incarcerated, a criminal is at least temporarily removed from society. However, incarceration does not always stop the crime; the tentacles of identity theft networks reach into the general prison populations, where criminals commit online credit card fraud to purchase merchandise that is delivered to outside accomplices, for kickbacks in money or drugs that are infiltrated back into the prison facility. Following release from prison, many criminals recidivate; should this be true for identity theft criminals, the cycle of identity crimes could be expected to resume. Despite all this, reactive legislation is necessary, to help victims resolve credit and other problems, such as clearing unwarranted criminal records. Of course, the best legislation would prevent the identity theft in the first place. Sometimes, however, reactive bills are precursors for proactive bills that come later when the crime is better understood. Examples are recent bills proposed in the state of California.

California has taken a lead in identity theft regulation, perhaps because it was the first state to report an insurgence of identity crimes. One lawmaker in particular, U.S. Senator Dianne Feinstein, has taken a leadership role in protecting "personal" information that includes bills that were first to link identity theft to terrorism and insider theft.[6] A recent amendment to the Identity Theft and Assumption Deterrence Act penalizes insiders who use their employment positions to commit fraud or help others commit fraud. Although not (yet) preventive, the bill is a beginning toward the real solution in which the legislation would be amended to require all businesses that use personal information to show evidence for "personnel selection for security" procedures that comply with Equal Employment Opportunity Commission (EEOC) Guidelines and Title VII statutes for fairness in personnel practices and that meet the standards of "information process" risk assessments.[7] Such legislation requiring security standards for people and processes would explicitly target insider theft prevention; coupled with current IT security requirements, such legislation would eliminate opportunities for identity theft, thereby decreasing or even preventing identity crimes. But as yet, there is no such legislation because, prior to the publication of this book (see Part II), there have been no such security standards. Thus, for this final and cumulative reason, identity crimes are predicted to increase greatly unless something is done very soon.

The burden of preventing identity thefts lies with businesses for two reasons:

1. The majority of identity thefts occur in the workplace.
2. Businesses are required by law to develop, document, and implement information security programs.

The problem is that those laws neither define what constitutes an information security program nor describe how a business would go about developing such a program. Nonetheless, as the laws discussed in Chapter 5 make clear, businesses must comply or face fines.

CHAPTER 5

LEGAL REQUIREMENTS FOR BUSINESSES

Businesses are required under several federal laws to develop, implement, and document evidence for "information security programs," or they risk being fined. But problems with the laws are innumerable: they are too broad and too flexible; they fail to cover "people" within businesses who are given access to personal information; and they do not concern the "work processes" the people perform, such as financial transactions using applications containing personal information. Moreover, the laws do not state *how* to develop the specified information security program and, except for expecting information technology (IT) to secure computers and networks, the laws do not provide uniform security standards.

This failure to require security standards is particularly problematic because, as discussed in Chapter 4, personal information is widely disseminated worldwide. Databases of information distributed around the world to second, third, and other parties are under no one's control and therefore are uncontrollable. Surprisingly, of the many laws enacted to prevent identity theft, not one contains provisions that actually would secure identities.

MANY LAWS

Five federal laws require information security, including the Fair Credit Reporting Act (FCRA), the Privacy Rule of the Federal Trade

40

Commission (FTC), the Banking Guidelines, the Health Insurance Portability and Accountability Act (HIPAA), and the Gramm-Leach-Bliley Safeguards Rule (GLB Act).[1] Additionally, the following federal agencies, collectively called the Federal Agencies, require businesses to keep personal information confidential: the U.S. Treasury's Office of the Comptroller of the Currency, Treasury (OCC); the Federal Reserve System's Board of Governors; the Federal Deposit Insurance Corporation (FDIC); and the Office of Thrift Supervision, Treasury (OTS).

Of all of these, the GLB Act, enacted on November 12, 1999, to reform the financial services industry, is the most comprehensive. The Gramm-Leach-Bliley Safeguards Rule, effective May 23, 2003, implemented the safeguards of the GLB Act. According to this Act, confidential information is defined as: any personal information given by an individual to obtain a financial, healthcare, or other product or service, including name, address, Social Security number, a mother's maiden name, bank account number, credit card or retail account number, driver's license information, or any other information on an application or used in any financial transaction. Further, the Act defines financial institutions as *"any entity that engages in any kind of financial activity"* and requires these institutions to *"develop information security programs"* (emphasis added) and also to train and designate employees to coordinate them.[2] However, nowhere does this or any other law stipulate what constitutes the required *information security program* or what is to be included in the training.

Instead, the act requires that institutions must:

1. Give customers privacy notices.
2. Provide customers opportunities to decline having their information shared with third parties.
3. Avoid releasing personal information to unauthorized users.
4. Assure accuracy of personal information before releasing it.
5. Disclose to the consumer recipients of any released information.
6. Identify internal and external risks to security.
7. Develop and implement information security programs.

Unfortunately, these requirements, even as detailed in the text of the act, are merely superficial.

MANY "SUPERFICIAL" LAWS

The federal laws that claim to provide security are neither inclusive nor exhaustive—they fail to address either "people" or "work processes," two major sources of identity theft, and the laws also neither describe nor prescribe any measures that actually would secure personal information. Additionally, ambiguities with each of the seven requirements render them ineffective. Specifically, the requirements of businesses to (1) give customers privacy notices raises more questions than answers and gives customers cause for concern. For example, some notices authorize access of personal information by *indirectly* related but unspecified businesses. Yes, businesses must also (2) provide consumers with opportunities to decline having their information shared with third parties—a reference to the "opt-out" choices that are only temporary because databases repeatedly are passed along to unaccountable, and sometimes indirectly related (and therefore unknown), other companies. Not only ambiguous, this requirement also is puzzling, as is the third, which (3) requires businesses to avoid releasing personal information to unauthorized users—that is, those not directly or (again) indirectly authorized.

Additionally, businesses are to (4) assure the accuracy of personal information before releasing it. As businesses are not required first to obtain from the customer notices of accuracy, how is accuracy determined? Only the customer knows the accuracy of the information, which is, after disseminated along a chain of second, third, and other parties, especially subject to deterioration, either intentional or inadvertent. A related but similarly confusing requirement is that businesses also are to (5) disclose to the consumer recipients of any released information; here again, once information is released to a business, it may subsequently be passed along to others who in turn release to others ad infinitum—also again, such business may be directly *and* indirectly related and thus unknown.

Finally, businesses are to (6) identify internal and external risks to security, and (7) develop and implement information security programs. How, exactly, are businesses supposed to identify internal and external risks? The laws do not answer this question, nor are businesses told how to develop the information security program, defined by Section 314.2 of the FTC's Final Rule as "the administrative, technical, or physical safeguards that a financial institution uses to access, collect, process, store, use, transmit, dispose of, or otherwise handle *customer* [emphasis added] information." Note that this definition does not cover the personal information of *employees*, which would include payroll, healthcare, benefits, and all other information that equates the employee's name with a Social Security number and other identifiers. No less than customers, employees are susceptible to identity theft and are as worthy of protection.

Additionally, neither these seven requirements nor any others specify the security of work processes, which must be a legislative oversight inasmuch as work processes are sources of stolen identities. Further, and in addition to all of the problems just mentioned, these broad laws with their pervasive omissions were intentionally written to be *flexible*—despite the established fact from the field of security management that *security* of anything requires comprehensive, firm, and distinctly delineated standards.

To further explain, the "flexibility" clauses of Section 314.3, FTC Standards for Safeguarding Customer Information, were specifically written so that small businesses could comply without incurring costly consultant fees and also so that the information security program would cover a "continuous life cycle" that, over time, can "meet the needs of a particular organization or industry." In short, businesses that can afford it may each comply with the laws, according to their needs. Thus, the laws require of businesses no universal standards for either people or work process security. And without universal standards for people and processes, there can be no security. Fortunately, there are solutions.

Personal information—identities—*can* be secured in businesses using inexpensive and universally applicable solutions that also are sufficiently comprehensive to bring businesses into compliance with all current as well as anticipated laws to be enacted in the future. The solutions are security standards developed using established and effective methods from industrial and organizational psychology, business management, and the field of criminal justice. Security standards developed using these methods comprise the information security program, or, more formally, the Business Information Security Program (BISP).

BISP SECURITY STANDARDS

Many businesses use universally accepted and widely documented methods from industrial and organizational psychology and the field of quality management to select *high-performing* employees who perform their work using *quality-driven processes*. These management methods, when adapted to *security management*, can select and develop *high-security* workforces that perform jobs using *security-developed work processes*. Security, as with quality, must center on both "people" and "*work* processes." The methods are straightforward and easy to implement.

People Security

Reputable personnel tests select job applicants for performance, motivation, and integrity. Other management methods socialize newly hired employees into honest company cultures that are developed using yet other established procedures. Thousands of businesses already use these tools that focus on "people" and "honest performance." For information security, the focus also is on "people" and "honest performance." The same industrial and organizational methods can be, and are effectively used in Part II of this book, to develop "people" standards of security. Not only are these methods valid (they measure what they purport to measure) and reliable (the measures are consistent), but they also are capable of increasing profits by reducing the monumental losses due to identity thefts.

These methods, moreover, are consistent and stable temporally, situationally, and organizationally, regardless of business size, type, or geographical location. This means that the people security standards are universally applicable, not only now but also over time and into the future as new laws are enacted. The technical industrial/organizational term describing this universal stability is "generalizability." And this generalizability is precisely what the FTC standards call for in Section 314.3 requiring information security programs to cover a "continuous life cycle" that over time will "meet the needs of a particular organization or industry."[3]

These flexible FTC standards intend in part to make security affordable for small businesses. But security is not cost prohibitive. For "people" security, the investments range from a few hundred to several thousand dollars, depending on the complexity of the business. The methods used for security are tangible, amortizable assets that can be used repeatedly; and they do not deteriorate, degrade, or otherwise become obsolete, for either people or work process security. In comparison, civil fines under the Health Insurance Portability and Accountability Act (HIPAA) are specified at up to $100 per violation, and criminal penalties range from $50,000 to $250,000 and from 1 to 10 years in prison. Work process security methods also are economical to develop and last as long as management is motivated to employ them.

Work Process Security

First used in the mid-1940s to establish and measure efficiency in manufacturing processes, "quality" standards are now required to ensure, for example, quality services, quality products, and, effective in 2005, the worldwide uniformity of bar codes. The quality process template has been made and refined over time. It is this template that established *quality in manufacturing processes* that now can be used to produce *security* in *work processes*. That is, the quality management methods can be applied to security management, because manufacturing processes are analogous to work processes. The only difference between the two is that "work" processes refer to white-collar job tasks, such as conducting financial transactions or assessments that require processing of personal and other information, whereas manufacturing processes refer to blue-collar jobs, such as assembly or product development that requires processing of materials. Both involve work processes.

These quality management methods, used together with information process risk assessments from the field of criminal justice, produce two results:

1. Information process risk assessments identify internal and external risks to security in work processes.
2. Once so identified, mechanisms and methods are developed to secure those processes.

Recall the sixth provision of the GLB Act: Businesses are to identify internal and external risks to security. Information process risk assessments can help businesses comply with this requirement.

These methods for people and process security, together with the already required IT provisions, can comprehensively secure personal information in any business, anywhere. These methods produce security standards that constitute a Business Information Security Program that meets and exceeds the current federal legal requirements by securing not only "customer" and "consumer" identities but also "employee" and "business" identities—the sum total of information vulnerable to identity theft. Furthermore, this BISP increases profits by reducing the monumental costs of identity theft and identity crimes. However, although the BISP presented (in Part II of this book) in lay language requires no special training or skills and is not cost prohibitive, its success is conditional. Before embarking on formulating an information security program, first consider the warnings and explanations given in Chapter 6.

CHAPTER 6

CAVEAT LECTOR: LET THE READER BEWARE

The information security program contained in Parts II and III of this book may not be for you. The program consists of a set of security standards that are guaranteed to prevent identity theft in all businesses regardless of size, type, or location, but developing and implementing these standards requires the time and interest of managers and employees. Another prerequisite, however, in addition to time and interest, is the *psychological* commitments of the chief executive officers—the *motivation* and *devotion* the CEOs give to the success of an information security program and the *support* they give to employees to help develop it.

The success of the program is, additionally, subject to the discipline and willingness of employee-manager teams working together. To develop and implement the information security program, teams must meet for up to four hours each week over several weeks to follow step-by-step and consecutively ordered exercises. The messages to executives and employees that follow may help to determine whether an information security program is feasible for your company at this time.

MESSAGE TO EXECUTIVES

This book is based on considerable research on crime in the workplace, conducted over a period of 15 years in public and private companies with hundreds of executives and employees; with criminals in 23 federal prisons across the United States; from investigations of identity theft crimes and networks; and, since 1999, from working with hundreds of identity theft victims. As you undoubtedly know (or you would not have purchased this book), no business is immune to crime in the workplace, especially the overarching crime of identity theft.

By the year 2005, an estimated 1.7 million people and an untold number of businesses will be victims of identity theft. The majority of these crimes will have been committed inside the workplace by a relatively few dishonest employees. These dishonest few threaten the security of your company's four most valuable assets:

1. Your *people*—the majority of honest and hardworking employees, current customers, and consumers you wish to attract
2. Your company's work *processes*—those sequential job tasks that comprise all job positions and through which personal information is evaluated, documented, maintained, and otherwise managed
3. *Proprietary information*—the personal information used in those work processes, without which your company cannot operate
4. Your *property*—the tools used to process the information, both real (computers, networks, and other digital systems) as well as virtual (Uniform Resource Locations [URLs], e-business Web sites, and e-mail addresses)

These four assets—people, processes, proprietary information, and property—can be protected from identity theft in your company, at little cost.

What are these costs? The greatest is the three- to four-hour workshops that must be held each consecutive week in which department managers and employees meet as a team to develop the security standards. The standards—the information security program—require a series of exercises that are to be completed in sequential order over several weeks. The number of weeks depends on the size of the department or departments to be secured and the complexity of the work processes—the series of job tasks that form the jobs within a department. In addition to the time involvement of the employee and manager team or teams (one team for each department), one of the exercises requires either focus group or individual interviews with other employees, officers, and other stakeholders. The cost in time for one focus group interview is estimated at one hour or less. All other costs are decision choices, some of which may involve either short- or long-term budgeting. Other than the time investment, most costs are relatively minimal. And for many of the security standards, there are no financial costs at all. In fact, the largest cost is not a dollar value but, rather, the psychological investment made by you, which will determine the success of the information security program.

You must approve, prioritize, and emphasize to your employees the importance *to you* of this information security program. (Employees themselves already recognize the need for security standards, as they want to feel safe within their own companies.) Your support for information security, and employee's concern for safeguards, is important. With executive support, employees tend to embrace and assume ownership in initiatives they help develop and implement. For the security standard initiative, the methods involved can be described succinctly in a few sentences.

Employee-manager teams working together complete a series of sequentially ordered exercises that are described in lay language and that require no special skills or training. Some exercises use tools from quality management and are already familiar to some employees. The exercises are structured so that each can be completed within three to four hours—the estimated time each consecutive week the team(s) must meet to complete each exercise. Once completed, the exercises in Parts II and III provide a set of security standards that will prevent identity thefts. The benefits include immediate and long-term dollar savings from:

- Fewer fraudulently purchased products and services
- Enhanced productivity of employees whose job tasks are not interrupted by their customers' or their own identity thefts

- Retaining customers who feel safe doing business with your company
- Attracting new customers who have been made aware of your company's information security program
- Protecting your own employees from threats of identity theft

An additional and very special benefit is the distinguished "Seal of Information Security" your company will receive from the Michigan State University–Business Identity Theft Partnerships in Prevention, at the annual awards ceremony. The Seal testifies that your company has implemented and enforces the security standards required by federal law and signifies to employees and customers alike that everything possible is being done to protect them.

The caveat, therefore, is this: The success of establishing an information security program in your company depends, first and foremost, on the highest-level executives—your sincere motivation and follow-through are essential. If this kind of leadership involvement is not now possible, then "now" may not be the time for you. If, however, you are so determined, then the Partnerships in Prevention—an outreach initiative at Michigan State University—will work with you and your employees to ensure success. You may call on the Partnership's management team to help you with any questions along the way. As a final step, the team will be happy to review your new information security program prior to implementation and in preparation for the annual awards ceremony.

MESSAGE TO EMPLOYEES

Although "business" identity theft is the latest crime trend, "personal" identity theft currently has reached epidemic proportions, which is why the first focus of identity theft prevention and control is on protecting "personal" identities. When it comes to safeguarding personal identities, employees, not upper management, hold the positions of authority. This is because employees who perform the job tasks that process personal information are also closest to the policies, practices, and procedures that can help prevent identity thefts. In fact, given management support, employees can develop, implement, and enforce security standards and, in effect, create and maintain an honest company culture where they can feel safe and secure.

The tools and methods used to develop these security standards for the workplace are adapted from "quality" management and also from other management sciences, including industrial and organizational psychology. For example, the workshop exercises involving *work process security* use quality management problem-solving tools—brainstorming, flow-charting, and cause-and-effect analysis—and the *people security* exercises use methods from industrial and organizational psychology. For all of the exercises, step-by-step instructions are provided and no special skills or previous training is required. For success, however, there are four conditions.

1. The exercises must be completed in the order in which they are presented in the chapters. The order of sequence *does* matter.

2. The exercises require department managers and employees to work together in teams for three to four hours each week for several consecutive weeks. (Earlier exercises may take longer to establish a learning curve.) Managerial involvement in these exercises is essential because managers must understand, accept, and approve of the specific security standards (there are options) the teams develop.

3. Each team is to consist of at least one, and preferably more than one, department manager together with two to four employees from that department. Large companies may have many departments and thus many teams, one for each department—comprehensive security standards require all departments be secured.

4. The team exercises must be completed consistently and in subsequent weeks by the same manager-employee team members. For some weekly exercises and for businesses with labor unions, the teams may involve bargaining unit members. The number of

weeks it takes to complete the exercises can range from several to 30 or more, depending on the size of the company, the number of departments, and the complexity of job tasks (the work processes) performed within a department.

In short, the four conditions for success require discipline. Team members must follow the steps in the exercises and follow the exercises consecutively, with each exercise building on the previous ones. Teamwork must last as long as it takes to develop and implement the information security program—the security standards.

Parts II and III of this book present the program. It begins in Chapter 7, which describes the four-factor model of security: people, processes, proprietary information, and property. The model is the foundation for security standards that, when integrated with the information technology security measures that most companies already have in place, provide for a comprehensive information security program. Part II describes the tools and methods used in the exercises to develop the program.

Your success in each of these chapters is important to me, which is why I give you my contact information at the ID Theft Crime and Research Lab: *idtheft@msu.edu*, (517) 432-4236. Someone from the Lab management team will respond to questions in as timely a manner as possible. And I hope to personally award your company the Seal of Business Information Security at the annual ceremony, where teams are invited to give brief presentations on their success stories. Let me know if you might be interested. Now, let's begin!

PART II

IDENTITY THEFT PREVENTION

Securatio populi suprema lex.

(The People's security is the highest law.)

Legal Maxim

CHAPTER 7

THE BISP PLAN: TIGHTEN YOUR BUSINESS BORDERS

L arge and small businesses alike, whether domestic, international, or multinational and regardless of service, product, or market, share in certain common assets.

BACKGROUND REVIEW: FOUR-FACTOR MODEL OF INFORMATION SECURITY

There are four valuable assets that all businesses share:

1. People (employees and customers)
2. Work processes
3. Proprietary information
4. Property

These four factors, or security fronts, are highly interdependently integrated: *people* in their work *processes* verify, validate, manage, and maintain "personal" and "business" *information* using business *properties*—both actual (computers) and virtual (e-business Web sites). This integrated interdependency across the four factors means that businesses must secure each factor in order to ultimately secure their business borders.

Conveniently, the Business Information Security Program (BISP) is universally applicable; that is, the methods and the exercises used to develop the Security Standards apply similarly to all types of businesses. The only difference businesses will experience in applying the BISP is the time required to complete each exercise: The greater the size and/or complexity of the company, the greater the time requirement. Nevertheless, even the largest and most complex business enterprise can afford the time required to secure its assets, beginning with the first front, the people.

People: The First Factor

The primary assets of every business are people: the employees who are and maintain the organization; the customers who support and sustain the organization; and the suppliers, vendors, contractors, shareholders, and other stakeholders, any of whom may have access to employee or customer identities. Throughout history, a relatively small percentage of people have committed crimes in the workplace against coworkers and customers. Examples are workplace violence and white-collar crimes of fraud and embezzlement. The twenty-first-century crime of identity theft adds another dimension—a relatively few dishonest insiders inflict emotional and financial pain and suffering on coworkers and customers by stealing and fraudulently using their identities.[1] These insiders may be temporary, contract, permanent, full-time, or part-time employees, or individuals impersonating employees— perpetrators who may hire into a company for the sole purpose of engaging in identity theft.

To protect the majority of U.S. workers and their customers from the threat of this insidious offense, the simple solution is to secure the entire personnel process, from recruitment, to selection, to organizational socialization and occupation. Only in this way can *people*—the employees and their customers alike—be secure in the marketplace. But businesses can be victims, too, and identity security involves the *process* front, where both "personal" and "business" identities can be threatened.

Processes: The Second Factor

Processes refer to the input-throughput-output of *information* on employees or customers as this information is processed in a department. Information, such as personal and business identities, is an asset that can be secured by securing the information processes—the sequence of job tasks performed on the information (identities). A process, for example, may be the sequence of tasks required to fill work orders or medical prescriptions, to conduct financial audits or prepare tax forms, to prepare employee payroll checks, to process credit card applications, or to establish retail credit accounts. For each of these, the job tasks expose names, addresses, Social Security numbers, tax identification numbers, and other personal and business information, or identities. Without such information, there would be no job tasks to perform: The jobs exist to *process* identifying information.

An example of a work process is taken from an actual case in which a major automaker leases automobiles to corporate managers. The process begins with the receipt of an application from a manager for the lease of an automobile, which arrives at the leasing department through company mail or by U.S. mail, e-mail, fax, or telephone. Upon receipt, the information on the application is verified against company records to confirm the applicant's job position with the company. Then the applicant's identifying data—name, Social Security number, and driver's license number—are verified with the state's driver's license bureau to check for violations and confirm validity of licensure. After all information has been verified and the application is approved, the company dealer is given authorization to release the automobile to the manager. From the point of entry into the department to the authorization to the company dealer, identity information is processed through a series of sequential job tasks in multiple job positions. Whether processed digitally or in paper format, there are many points, links, or places within and between the steps in this process in which identity information can be pilfered. The Information Process Risk Assessment (Chapter 18) is the BISP method used to secure proprietary information in all types of work processes and for any type of business.

Proprietary Information: The Third Factor

Proprietary information—the third factor—is a business asset that is integrated into each of the other three factors in the model: people, processes, and property. Technically, proprietary information is any confidential business information including marketing objectives, product designs, business plans, and any other information related, either directly or indirectly, to the profits earned by the sale of a company's products or services, including employee, customer, and business identities. Although the BISP focuses entirely on protecting the "identity" form of proprietary information, BISP methods can be used, in follow-up exercises, to secure *all* proprietary information. Regardless of the type, all proprietary information can be secured by securing the *people, processes,* and *property.*

Property: The Fourth Factor

The term "property" refers to tangible or intangible lawfully owned possessions of the business, including property within the company's physical boundaries as well as the unbounded virtual properties. Tangible property includes the physical structures and surrounding grounds, computer, network, and other electronic communication systems and other equipment and materials used to conduct the business. The tangible properties of primary interest in these exercises are fax machines, landline telephones, and cell phones; employee and company mailboxes; desks, and file drawers; and the physical organization of job stations (positions) within a department. Tangible properties also include computers and any technology used to transmit, store, or process identity data. Many books and articles have been written on computer and network security. There are laws in place establishing security standards for this information technology. Methods to develop these (computer) standards, although not part of the BISP, are essential for comprehensive identity theft security, in combination with person, process, proprietary information, and property security.

The intangible property of specific interest here is the e-business Web site that operates in cyberspace. The concern in *Preventing Identity Theft in Your Business* is Web site security *from the perspective of the customer*. How secure does a consumer feel in submitting personal identities to *your* e-business Web site? The customer, whether on site or online, makes the final call as to whether to do business or not. To secure a business from identity thefts, the *people* (employees), their work *processes*, and the identifying *information* used in those processes must be secured, *and customers must recognize this security*. In later chapters, BISP exercises are conducted to develop a standard to measure and assess consumer perceptions of security when visiting your company online.

SECURING THE FRONTS

Securing the People Factor

In Chapter 8, exercises for Standards 1 and 2 will establish the basis for security by identifying your company's personal and business identities, their sources or entry-points into a department, and the internal and external jobs that use them. In subsequent chapters, standards will be developed to address *people* security, for it is the people—the employees and their customers—whose identities are stolen, and employees can be the first line of defense when it comes to threats to "information" security and identity theft.

The BISP uses the tools of quality management together with the methods of industrial and organizational psychology to secure the entire personnel function, thereby securing the *people*. Traditional methods designed to analyze jobs and then to recruit, screen, and select job applicants no longer are adequate for twenty-first-century business performance—security now must be incorporated into the traditional methods. When performed in the listed sequential order as described in these chapters, traditional personnel methods can be adapted to meet present-day challenges to attract and develop a high-performing workforce that is also secured from dishonest infiltrators. After the selection of job applicants, the next exercises develop standards for "organizational socialization" and to establish a "company culture of security." Thereafter, the team is guided through a series of exercises to develop the organizational feedback system whereby performance is evaluated at the organizational versus individual level of analysis.

The *people* factor and the exercises to develop standards for people security are targeted toward job positions of security—those jobs for which the job tasks are related to the security of proprietary and confidential information. The exercises are based on scientific research and real-world applications with documented evidence for the reliability and validity of the results. When used for positions of security, the personnel practices fully comply with the Equal Employment Opportunity Commission Guidelines and the Title VII statutes for fairness in personnel practices.[2]

Securing the Process Factor

After people security, the focus is directed toward the work process factor. The exercises for work process security and the information process risk assessment use, in part, the results from exercises conducted in the chapters on people security. There are, in addition, other important identity theft-related processes to consider, such as the e-shopping practices of consumers; customer service practices and processes; and legislative processes that may inhibit, prohibit, or promote financial transactions. Therefore, the exercises in Part III develop Security Standards for each of these consumer and legislative practices or processes. The fourth factor, after process security, is property security.

Securing the Property Factor

The property is the intangible e-business Web site described earlier. Businesses increasingly depend on cybertransactions to remain competitive; even the largest department stores now have online catalogs listing thousands of products and services and use Web site announcements to promote them. But consumers, also increasingly, are reluctant to shop online—the risk of identity theft has scared many away. However, online shopping is as safe as shopping at the local mall provided the consumer deals with reputable businesses and uses some practical e-shopping rules—these are the "best practices" described in Chapter 21 on e-commerce processes. However, the *overriding* "best practices" are the Security Standards developed to secure the integrated and interdependent four factors (people, processes, property, and, thereby, proprietary information) so as to prevent identity theft.

CHAPTER 8

BEGIN THE EXERCISES: IDENTIFY YOUR BUSINESS IDENTITIES

As described in Chapter 7, the Four-Factor Model of Information Security is the guiding framework for the systematic procedures used by the Business Information Security Program (BISP) to secure *your* business's identities. Recall also that all threats to information security and all information security solutions involve four valuable business assets:

1. People
2. Work processes
3. Proprietary information
4. Property (virtual and actual)

The BISP secures these four fronts through standards developed in a series of exercises sequenced throughout Chapters 8 to 22. Conveniently, all businesses can utilize the same exercises to establish and maintain security.

There is one end product for each standard: a security document or report. The resultant set of documents or reports are the Security Standards that collectively comprise the Business Information Security Program. By the time a business completes all the exercises in the chapters, it will have its own distinctive BISP because, even though the exercises and the standards are uniform for all businesses, the tangible end products—the security documents—are specific to the characteristics of job positions and work processes unique to each business.

The format for the exercises is consistent throughout the chapters: first, the goals are stated, then the objectives are specified, and, last, background information in the form of an orientation describes the requirements for conducting the exercises. For example, the orientation for the exercises to develop Standard 1 describes the requirements for the team composition and the method for electing a team and also gives instructions for using three quality-to-security management tools.[1] Although these instructions plus additional ones in Chapter 9 are lengthy, they are essential for the successful completion of all of the exercises throughout this book. Please note: These instructions are not repeated in successive chapters.

Except for this chapter, in which two standards are developed, subsequent chapters are comprised of one or more exercises that develop one security standard. The results of each chapter are used to complete the exercises in successive chapters. A summary conclusion at the end of each chapter reviews what is required or what is to have been completed before the team moves on to the next chapter's exercises.

The amount of time required to complete a chapter's exercises depends on the size of the department and the number of different job positions within that department. However, a benchmark time is given at the beginning of each exercise, based on actual exercises conducted with companies having departments of various sizes. It is important to strive to complete each exercise within the estimated time range. Appendix A provides a Security Standard Checklist on which to monitor completion of exercises for each standard.

This chapter begins by identifying the "personal" *and* "business" identities in your company and continues with related exercises to identify "internal" and "external" job positions that use these identities to perform job tasks. It provides the foundation for the Four-Factor Model of Information Security, the model that, in the remaining chapters, secure people, processes, and property. Let's begin!

STANDARD 1. WHAT ARE YOUR BUSINESS IDENTITIES?

Goals: Create two independent lists of identities (personal and business, exercises 1 and 3 below) as well as two correlating lists (exercises 2 and 4 below) showing the entry points of these identities into your department, in this order:

Exercise 1. Identify "personal" identities.
Exercise 2. Organize "personal" identities and determine entry points.
Exercise 3. Identify "business" identities.
Exercise 4. Organize "business" identities and determine entry points.

Specific Objectives: Create the above four lists using the team approach and two quality management problem-solving tools—formal brainstorming and cause-and-effect analysis. These lists prepare the foundation for securing the four fronts: people, processes, proprietary information, and property.

Orientation

Orientation consists of three steps:

1. Create the project team.
2. Review the definitions given in Chapter 1 for personal and business identities.
3. Carefully read the instructions, introduced below, for using the quality management tools.

Begin with Step 1.

Step 1. Create a project team of volunteered, selected, or elected employees who, with input from other company employees, will develop the security standards. The team is to be composed of a minimum of three and a maximum of five employees, including at least one manager. Team members are to be from the same department or from related (interdependent or cross-functional) departments. Each team member is to hold a different job position because the BISP exercises require a breadth of knowledge about the jobs and job tasks within a department. However, it is not necessary to represent all job positions within a department. Team members should be longer-tenured employees who, relative to more recent hires, have superior knowledge of the business, its jobs, and its work processes. When assembling this team, and for continuity, identify employees whose job positions are most likely to enable them to meet consistently at the same time and the same day each week throughout the several weeks of the project.

The exercises for all chapters are to be completed by the same team. For comprehensive security, the people, processes, proprietary information, and property for all company departments must be secured. However, the BISP can be rolled out consecutively by department or concurrently developed by multiple departments, each with its own team. Small businesses with few employees may require only one team to secure the four fronts for the entire business. Appendix B provides a checklist of team prerequisites. Take time now to review Appendix B, then create your team.

Step 2. Once the team is in place, begin by reviewing the types of "personal" and "business" identities described in those sections in Chapter 1. Notice that the identities include the confidential information of employees, customers, and the business itself. In the present Chapter 8, the team will conduct separate exercises to identify the personal and the business identities. However, the identities to be secured may differ depending on the department. For example, the exercises for a human resources department may focus strictly on employee identities; the exercises for another department may focus only on customer and not employee identities.

Step 3. Start creating your lists. Exercise 1 and others use formal brainstorming. Exercise 1 generates a list of identities used in departmental work processes. Some team members may be familiar with brainstorming as a problem-solving tool. There are, however, many brainstorming approaches, and some are more or less structured. For the BISP, the brainstorming is highly structured and formal. It is important to guard against relaxing this simple tool because deviations will fail to produce the results needed for security. Appendix C gives detailed and step-by-step instructions for conducting formal brainstorming. Also, Exhibit C.1 shows a sample brainstorming task statement created by a team working on a bioterrorism contingency plan, and Exhibit C.2 lists the results of a formal brainstorming session conducted by a team at the headquarters of a major automaker in Detroit. At this time, carefully read the instructions in Exhibits C.1 and C.2. Now begin with exercise 1.

Exercise 1. Identify "Personal" Identities

Estimated Time: One–Two Hours
This exercise exemplifies why employees are the best and perhaps the only individuals capable of securing confidential business information. A team of employees from the same department, each of whom holds a different job position, knows the content of the work performed within the department. Working together and using formalized procedures, the team members can identify the types of personal identities used in those work processes or that are otherwise accessible to the job positions.

Use structured and formal brainstorming according to the instructions in Appendix C. Generate a comprehensive list of the *types* of personal identities accessible to or used in work processes within your department. Your first "task statement" on the flip chart might be: Determine the types of identities used in work processes in our department. (Exhibit C.1 provides a sample task statement.) When conducting the brainstorming, consider any personal information that identifies employees or customers. Include any personal identifier, such as bank account numbers, credit card numbers, Social Security numbers, and employee identification numbers.

Write your task statement on a large flip chart to provide the central focus of attention. When noting a form of identity on the flip chart, use general terms such as "credit card numbers" and "bank account numbers," not the actual account (or other) numbers. Strive to complete this exercise within the time range. Then continue with exercise 2.

Exercise 2. Organize "Personal" Identities and Determine Entry Points

Estimated Time: One–Two Hours
Using the list of personal identities generated in exercise 1, now conduct cause-and-effect analysis to build on and organize this list. The goal is to categorize the personal identities according to their sources of entry into the department. These entry points will be secured in a later exercise. Conduct the cause-and-effect analysis (the second quality management tool) according to the specific BISP instructions described in Appendix D. Exhibits D.1 and D.2 show an example of the cause-and-effect framework. Before conducting the cause-and-effect analysis, carefully read Appendix D and review Exhibits D.1 and D.2.

Exercise 3. Identify "Business" Identities

Estimated Time: One–Two Hours
Follow the instructions in Appendix C for structured and formal brainstorming to generate an exhaustive list of the type of "business" identities accessible to, or used in, work processes within the team's department. The team will use these *business* identities in subsequent exercises.

Exercise 4. Organize "Business" Identities and Determine Entry Points

Estimated Time: One–Two Hours
Using the list of business identities generated in exercise 3, now conduct cause-and-effect analysis to categorize the identities according to their sources of entry into the department. Follow the specific instructions in Appendix D required by the BISP for conducting cause-and-effect analysis.

Summary

In exercises 1 to 4, two lists of identities were developed—a list of personal identities and a list of business identities. In addition, two other lists were developed showing the sources of these identities—personal and business. If all four lists have now been developed, then check off the completed exercises under Standard 1 on the Security Standard Checklist (Appendix A) and move on to Standard 2. Standards 1 and 2 together form the basis for the exercises in subsequent chapters.

STANDARD 2. WHO HAS ACCESS TO YOUR BUSINESS IDENTITIES?

Goals: First, identify both "internal" and "external" job positions that require knowledge of "personal" and "business" identities—credit card or bank account numbers, Social Security numbers, pass codes, and others. Then match the personal and business identities with the internal and external job positions that have access to those identities, as follows:

> Exercise 1. Determine "internal" job titles.
> Exercise 2. Match "internal" job titles with "personal" and "business" identities.
> Exercise 3. Determine "external" job titles.
> Exercise 4. Match "external" job titles with "personal" and "business" identities.

Specific Objectives: Use brainstorming, organizational charts and, if they are available, job descriptions, along with a one-hour focus group interview, to help pinpoint job positions that require access to identities. Later, the team will develop Security Standards for the work processes for those security-related job positions. The brainstorming is to be formally conducted by the team in the usual way; the organizational chart may show departmental job positions and titles; the job description may list job tasks that the team may be able to determine require access to identities; and the focus interview with other departmental employees may provide incremental and important information, and serves to integrate those employees into the BISP initiative.

Orientation

The BISP requires a specific focus group interview approach. Appendix E provides the details and step-by-step instructions on how to organize and conduct BISP focus group interviews. Carefully read the instructions in Appendix E, then continue with exercise 1.

Exercise 1. Determine "Internal" Job Titles

Estimated Time: One–Two Hours
Obtain the organization chart and also the departmental job descriptions for the jobs within the department, if available. Working from these documents and from team members' knowledge of the jobs within the department, conduct structured and formal brainstorming, using the strict BISP approach (Appendix C). First create the task statement and then generate a complete list of the job titles for all jobs *within* the department—these are the internal job titles. This list will be used in exercise 2, for the focus group interview.

Exercise 2. Match "Internal" Job Titles with "Personal" and "Business" Identities

Estimated Time: One–Two Hours
Use the list of job titles from exercise 1 for the BISP focus group interview. The goal, using the focus group interview, is to match the *types* of "personal" identities and "business" identities, such as bank account number, credit card number, Social Security number, tax identification number, or other, with job tasks for *each job title*. In preparation for the focus group interview, follow the directions in Appendix E and:

- Randomly select up to eight employees.
- Elect one team member to ask "questions" or "prompt" employees to help trigger their knowledge of the *types* of identities used in the various departmental job positions, referred to by the job titles.
- Elect a team "recorder" to list responses on the flip chart.

Other team members participate in the interview by generating new prompts triggered by employees' responses.

Conduct the focus group interview in two 30-minute stages:

1. Match "internal" job titles with "personal" identities.
2. Match "internal" job titles with "business" identities.

To begin, emphasize to employees that the "focus" of the group interview is on the job and not the person who performs a job. Explain also that the purpose of this group interview, and subsequent BISP exercises, is to involve all employees by obtaining their opinions on information that will help secure the company's people and work processes from threats of identity theft.

Exercise 3. Determine "External" Job Titles

Estimated Time: One–Two Hours

The present goal is to identify "external" job positions (referred to hereafter by their specific job titles) having access to "personal" and "business" identities, using the team approach and structured brainstorming. External job titles are those held by suppliers, vendors, database management companies, and other second and third parties. Specific examples are computer supplier, printer repairperson, call center agent, office cleaning contractor, office supply salesperson, invoice billing agent, database processor, and so on. Business transactions with external parties provide a conduit through which identities can cross business borders. In order to secure the pipeline, the team must identify those specific external parties. The first step, therefore, is to identify the external job titles. The second step is to match those job titles with the types of identities accessible by those jobs.

To prepare for the brainstorming session, obtain from the accounting department the names of vendors, suppliers, contractors, outsourcing companies, and other external entities. Working from this and other information, now use the team approach and structured brainstorming to generate a comprehensive list of external job titles involved in business transactions with your company. Use the flip chart with a task statement. As always, refrain from using the names of individuals holding those external jobs but refer instead to the job titles. For these job titles, you may also associate the company names (e.g., Johnson Company vendor). When the complete list of external job titles has been generated, move on to exercise 4.

Exercise 4. Match "External" Job Titles with "Personal" and "Business" Identities

Estimated Time: One–Two Hours
Now match the list of external job titles with the types of identities accessible to those jobs. Use the list of job titles generated in exercise 3 for a second focus group interview with a second, randomly generated group of eight departmental employees. Select as participants employees not involved in the first focus interview so as to obtain perspectives from a wide range of employees and to include as many employees in the overall project as possible. To prepare, elect a team member to give the "prompts" that will help employees trigger knowledge of the *types* of identities used by the various external job positions. Also elect a team "recorder" to itemize the responses on the flip chart with the task statement (Appendix E). Other team members participate by generating new prompts triggered from responses.

Conduct the focus group interview in two 30-minute stages, matching the external job titles first with "personal" identities and then with "business" identities. Emphasize that the focus is on the external jobs and not the individuals who perform those jobs. Explain also that the aim is to involve all employees in the development of the BISP by obtaining their opinions on information that will help throughout the project to secure the company from threats of identity theft.

Summary

In this chapter, Standards 1 and 2 were developed. For Standard 1, four lists were generated: two lists to identify "internal" and "external" job titles, and two lists to identify their sources into the department. Similarly, for Standard 2, four lists were developed: two lists of internal and external job titles, and two related lists that match the titles with specific types of "personal" as well as "business" identities. Use the checklist in Appendix A to record the completion of these exercises.

Through these exercises, the team now knows the:

- Types of personal and business identities used in departmental job tasks
- Sources of entry of those identities into the department
- Specific internal and external job positions that require access to identities
- Types of personal and business identities accessible by those job positions

This *company-specific* information is the basis of the four-factor model of information security, the guiding framework used in each chapter that follows, to create the standards that tighten *your* business borders.

CHAPTER 9

SECURING THE PEOPLE FRONT: THE SECURITY JOB ANALYSIS

For the Business Information Security Program (BISP), personnel decisions, from recruitment, to selection, to promotion or demotion, are all based on the results of a formally conducted "job analysis" that uses systematic procedures to comply with Equal Employment Opportunity Commission (EEOC) and Title VII statutes. The unit of analysis is the job, *not the job incumbent*. Companies that fail to conduct job analyses are exposed to liability in the event of charges of discrimination in personnel practices. This is because the job analysis identifies and describes the tasks performed on a job, and ultimately all personnel decisions are based on the performance of those job tasks. From determining pay ranges, to recruiting and testing the qualifications of job applicants, the overriding purpose is to select the highest-performing job applicants—those who can best perform the tasks identified by the job analysis. Yet many companies do not conduct job analyses, out of a mistaken belief that doing so is too costly or because of misunderstandings about the purpose and procedures.

Indeed, there is confusion about the job analytic procedure, perhaps because, over the years, researchers have discovered new approaches and techniques that have added new language and methods to a once-basic traditional procedure (which, nevertheless, still complies with legal statutes). Today, terms associated with job analysis, such as "knowledge," "skills," "abilities," "traits," "attributes," "behavior," "competencies," and "tasks," have complicated the literature and confused some companies. For example, a job "task" is a specific job "behavior" that, when more broadly defined, is sometimes now called a job "competency." There are also misunderstandings about the procedure itself. For example, job "analysis" often is used interchangeably (and mistakenly) with job "evaluation"; however, the terms are not synonymous. The unit of analysis for job analysis is the job, whereas the job incumbent is the unit of analysis for a job evaluation. Additionally, many sometimes complex variations exist on *how* to conduct a job analysis, not all of which, unfortunately, meet the EEOC requirements. The traditional job analysis, however, is straightforward, and the tasks performed on a job can be identified in three easy-to-conduct steps: (1) interview, (2) observe, and (3) survey the job incumbent on the job tasks he or she performs.

The security job analysis follows the step-by-step instructions of this traditional approach with one additional short step to identify jobs that are security-sensitive—those jobs that use or have access to personal and business identifying information. Those jobs also are considered positions of security and authority, because those jobs are given access to personal or business identities, or both. These are the jobs to which the security standards apply. The security job analysis, therefore, without complexities or confusions and using a method applicable to any job in any business, brings the traditional job analysis up to twenty-first-century security standards.

STANDARD 3. SCIENTIFIC JOB ANALYSIS FOR SECURITY DECISION MAKING

Goals: Determine the security-relatedness of jobs within the department.

Specific Objectives: Incorporate into the traditional job analysis a security-sensitive component to identify job tasks for jobs within the department that use or have access to either personal or business identifying information, in compliance with EEOC Guidelines and Title VII statutes for fairness in personnel practices.

Orientation

The preparation for the job analysis requires:

1. A review of laws pertinent to the "traditional" job analysis
2. A team composition unique for this standard only
3. Knowledge of a few technical terms
4. Identification of departmental job "sets"—jobs having similar or identical job tasks—by using existing job descriptions, if available

Step 1. Review the laws. Under Title VII of the Civil Rights Act of 1964 and the U.S. Equal Employment Opportunity Commission's Uniform Guidelines[1] on Employee Selection Procedures, employment practices must be job related and consistent with business necessity. Employment practices include recruitment, testing, hiring, promotion, transfer, and firing. Personnel decisions, according to these laws, must be related to the tasks performed on the job, and tasks on the job are determined by conducting a thorough job analysis. The BISP and the security standards require a security job analysis to determine whether "security" is a job-related component. This step provides the team with relevant and essential background information on the laws required for job analysis. Team members should carefully read and then review as a team the Title VII regulations for personnel practices. For each item listed, the Web site link is provided.

(i) Who is covered?

The Uniform Guidelines cover ... all private employers, state and local governments, and education institutions that employ 15 or more individuals. These laws also cover private and public employment agencies, labor organizations, and joint labor management committees controlling apprenticeship and training.

Review these requirements at *www.eeoc.gov/policy/vii.html*

(ii) What employment practices are covered?

The Uniform Guidelines on Employee Selection Procedures (1978) apply to tests and other selection procedures which are used as a basis for any employment *decision* [emphasis added]. Employment decisions include but are not limited to hiring, promotion, demotion, membership (for example, in a labor organization), referral, retention, and licensing and certification, to the extent that licensing and certification may be covered by Federal equal employment opportunity law. Other selection decisions, such as selection for training or transfer, may also be considered employment decisions if they lead to any of the decisions listed above.

> Review these requirements under "Scope. Sec. 1607.2 (B)" at
> *www.access.gpo.gov/nara/cfr/waisidx_03/29cfr1607_03.html*

(iii) How the law defines job analysis

Under the Uniform Guidelines, a job analysis should describe all important work behaviors, their relative importance, and their difficulty level. [A] job analysis [should include] an analysis of the important work behavior(s) required for successful performance and their relative importance and, if the behavior results in work product(s), an analysis of the work product(s). Any job analysis should focus on the work behavior(s) and the tasks associated with them. If work behavior(s) are not observable, the job analysis should identify and analyze those aspects of the behavior(s) that can be observed and the observed work products. The work behavior(s) selected for measurement should be critical work behavior(s) and/or important work behavior(s) constituting most of the job.

> Review Technical Standards for validity studies, Section 1607.4
> at *www.access.gpo.gov/nara/cfr/waisidx_03/29cfr1607_03.html*

Step 2. Create unique subteams. The job analysis requires a unique team composition: For a department with more than one job "set" (defined in step 3), the job analysis is to be conducted by team "pairs." Unlike other exercises where the team works together, a security job analysis is conducted most effectively by dividing the team into smaller groups, each of which will analyze one or more job sets. For example, for most departments and with a team of five employees and one manager, three pairs can analyze all departmental jobs quickly and efficiently. All team pairs use the same exercises and step-by-step instructions. Select the team pairs now.

Step 3. Know the terms. Carefully review and be able to distinguish the following terms:

- The term "job set" is used interchangeably with "job family" to define groups of jobs that consist of the same or similar job tasks. Examples are secretarial jobs where the primary tasks are answering phones, scheduling appointments, and performing word processing tasks; and the job of data processor where the data being processed may be different for different jobs but the actual task of processing is the same or similar.
- A job "task" is a *specific* job "behavior" or job "action." When broadly defined, "general" or "technical" job tasks are sometimes called "competencies."
- A "general" competency can be "generalized" across jobs. For example, "general" competencies such as timeliness (a behavior), accuracy (an action), and honesty (a characteristic) are required of most job tasks and most jobs, regardless of rank or description. (A *specific* job task for the general competency term "timeliness" might be to "write and submit a report on or before the last day of each month.")
- A "technical" competency refers to a special set of requirements for performing a certain job. Technical competencies also may be the same or similar across jobs, but to a lesser extent than for general competencies. Examples of technical competencies are "using word processing programs" or "creating programs using a variety of database languages." (A *specific* job task for the technical competency "using various word processing programs" might simply be "prepare a report on the annual meeting using the MSWord software program.")

- Knowledge, Skills, and Abilities (KSAs) are three words sometimes used in the context of job analysis. Knowledge is passive information about some subject; skills are learned; and abilities are the innate aptitudes to learn the skills. These terms are used later to help describe job tasks.
- Job "characteristics" describe the nature of the job: Examples are exactness, accuracy, timeliness, and consistency. Take the time to review the comprehensive list of job characteristics online at the Occupational Information Network (O*NET) located at *http://online.onetcenter.org.*
- "Security-sensitive" is the single term that is used to describe general and technical job competencies that directly or indirectly involve personal or business identifying information.

Most jobs require both technical and general competencies. For example, the job tasks for finance and accounting jobs may require competencies to "perform mathematical and accounting operations," "conduct specialized fraud audits," or "secure proprietary documents." These competencies are very specific. In contrast, the same job tasks might require the *general* competencies to "attend to detail" and "perform the job tasks with accuracy." Readers will be able to distinguish these terms easily after they are introduced in successive exercises, following orientation step 4.

Step 4. Determine job sets. This step, preliminary to the job analysis, requires all members of the team to work together. Determine job sets within the department using current job descriptions, if available, and if based on the traditional form of job analysis that meets EEOC and Title VII requirements. Review the job descriptions for jobs that share in common similar or the same job tasks. Using the job titles, group these jobs together to form the job set. The job analysis will be conducted on job sets, if identified, and also on individual jobs not amenable to grouping. If the grouping of a job is in question, discuss and agree by consensus whether that job should be considered a member of the set. *Upon completion of step 4, begin the job analysis.*

Exercise 1. Identify Job Tasks

Estimated Time: Three–Four Hours
This three-step exercise develops lists of job tasks.

1. List the specific job tasks for the job sets and for each job not grouped into a job set, using the above job descriptions, if available.
2. Interview the current job incumbent or, for job sets, the incumbents. Job incumbents are the job's subject matter experts—these employees know best what tasks are performed on their jobs. Simply ask the incumbent to tell you about the job; that is, on a day-to-day basis: What are the job tasks you perform? What knowledge or special skills are required? What types of equipment are used? What are the characteristics of this job—do the tasks require exactness, accuracy, timeliness, consistency, or some other "job" characteristics? Make notes and use a recorder. Immediately after the interview or soon thereafter, transcribe the notes into a list of the job tasks for that job.
3. On a separate occasion, observe as unobtrusively as possible the job incumbent(s) while they perform their job(s). Arrange a one-hour block of observation time and explain in advance your purpose. While observing, simply write down your observations in a notebook. Do not ask questions or interact with an incumbent at this time. Focus on the job task being performed and jot down in simple terms *what* you observe being done (word processing, analyzing, climbing a ladder, leading); *why* it is being done, if apparent (to prepare a document, reconcile an accounting statement, change a light fixture, show other employees some technique); *how* it is being done (standing, sitting, stooping, reaching); and the equipment used (computer, software, calculator, ladder). If it is a "shift" job, different tasks may be performed on different shifts; in this case, it is necessary to interview and also observe incumbents *for each shift*. As soon as possible after the observation, review and compile from your notes a list of the tasks you observed being performed.

You now have three lists of job tasks with details about how those tasks are performed: one list from the job description, a second from the incumbent interview, and a third from your own observation. Now *consolidate* these three lists: For each job or job set, sort the job tasks into one of two categories: technical or general. Completing this step forms the base of the job analysis for the remaining, relatively shorter exercises. Exercise 2, in compliance with EEOC Guidelines, determines how *essential* the job tasks are for each job or job set. Begin exercise 2 now.

Exercise 2. Create a Checklist of Job Tasks

Estimated Time: Three Hours

The Uniform Guidelines pertain to job tasks that are *essential* to the job, and *essentialness* is determined by the extent to which the job tasks are *important* for the job and how *frequently* those tasks are performed. In addition, a third component essential for the security standards is the extent to which each task is *security-sensitive*. This exercise creates a single checklist composed of these three major sections—importance, frequency, and security-sensitivity. In exercise 3, this checklist is administered to the subject matter experts—the job incumbents. Exhibit 9.1 shows an example of such a checklist, sometimes called a "job competency checklist." Use Exhibit 9.1 as a model: For each job (or job set), list the job title, then create two subheadings in the left column—one titled "technical" and the other titled "general." Now use the list from exercise 1 to itemize each job task accordingly as either a technical or general job task. Although the exhibit shows only a few job tasks, most jobs have many more. In the right column, for each major section (technical and general), note the rating scale of 1 (low) to 5 (high). The job incumbent will use this scale later to rate each job task according to its relative importance, frequency, and job sensitivity. Continuing with exercise 2, in the right-hand column and after each task, create the 1-to-5 rating scale as in Exhibit 9.1. Be sure to include the rating keys at the bottom of the scale:

- For *importance*: 1 = not important, 2 = somewhat important, 3 = important, 4 = very important, and 5 = critically important
- For *frequency*: 1 = never, 2 = sometimes, 3 = occasionally, 4 = often, 5 = most frequently
- For *security-sensitivity*: 1 = does not use or have access to personal or business identifying information; 2 = uses or has access to personal or business identifying information

EXHIBIT 9.1 *Job Competency Checklist for Job of Computer Forensic Analyst*

Competencies	Importance to Job				
	Circle Only *One* Response				
Technical					
1. Computer hardware certification	1	2	3	4	5
2. Skills to secure computer databases	1	2	3	4	5
3. Ability to detect security intrusions	1	2	3	4	5
4. Knowledge of information risk assessments	1	2	3	4	5
5. Ability to maintain security standards	1	2	3	4	5
6. Knowledge of identity theft and crimes	1	2	3	4	5
7. Job tasks involving employee identities	1	2	3	4	5
8. Job tasks involving customer identities	1	2	3	4	5
9. Job tasks involving business identities	1	2	3	4	5
General					
10. Honesty	1	2	3	4	5
11. Consistency	1	2	3	4	5
12. Integrity	1	2	3	4	5
13. Interpersonal skills	1	2	3	4	5
14. Accuracy	1	2	3	4	5
15. Timeliness	1	2	3	4	5

Key: 1 = not important, 2 = somewhat important, 3 = important, 4 = very important, 5 = critically important

(continues)

Competencies	Frequency of Job Performance				
	Circle Only *One* Response				

Technical

1.	Computer hardware and software certification	1	2	3	4	5
2.	Skills to secure computer databases	1	2	3	4	5
3.	Ability to detect security intrusions	1	2	3	4	5
4.	Conducting information process risk assessments	1	2	3	4	5
5.	Assessing compliance with Security Standards	1	2	3	4	5
6.	Knowledge of identity theft and crimes	1	2	3	4	5
7.	Job tasks involving employee identities	1	2	3	4	5
8.	Job tasks involving customer identities	1	2	3	4	5
9.	Job tasks involving business identities	1	2	3	4	5

General

10.	Honesty	1	2	3	4	5
11.	Consistency	1	2	3	4	5
12.	Integrity	1	2	3	4	5
13.	Interpersonal skills	1	2	3	4	5
14.	Accuracy	1	2	3	4	5
15.	Timeliness	1	2	3	4	5

Key: 1 = never, 2 = sometimes, 3 = occasionally, 4 = often, 5 = most frequently

JOB COMPETENCY CHECKLIST FOR JOB OF COMPUTER FORENSIC

Competencies	The Job Task Is Security Sensitive	
	Circle Only *One* Response	

Technical

1.	Computer hardware and software	1	2
2.	Securing computer databases	1	2

(continues)

Competencies	The Job Task Is Security Sensitive	
	Circle Only *One* Response	
3. Detecting security intrusions	1	2
4. Conducting information process risk assessments	1	2
5. Analyzing Security Standards for compliance	1	2
6. Recognizing identity thefts and identity crimes	1	2
7. Performing tasks involving employee identities	1	2
8. Performing tasks involving customer identities	1	2
9. Performing tasks involving business identities	1	2

Key: 1 = does not use or have access to personal or business identifying information
2 = occasionally or frequently uses or has access to personal or business identifying information

Exercise 3. Administer Checklist to Incumbent Expert(s)

Estimated Time: Two Hours
Employees are the job experts and, as in the other BISP exercises, they must play a major role in the job analysis. More than anyone else, job incumbents know which of their tasks are the most important and the most frequently performed. Solicit the employee-experts to rate their jobs using the checklist prepared in exercise 2.

Exercise 4. Score Checklist

Estimated Time: Two Hours
Now score the checklist; that is, simply rank-order the job tasks according to their rated importance (5 = most important), frequency (5 = most frequent), and sensitivity (1 = not sensitive; 2 = sensitive). The higher importance and most frequently rated job tasks are *essential* for that job, and a sensitive rating for one or more job tasks requires that that job be secured as a position of security and authority. (Regarding job task frequency, even though a frequently performed job task is rated as lesser in importance relative to some others, nonetheless the job task may be essential. For example, a job may require frequent monitoring of

e-mail messages, of which only a few may be for product orders, because for high-priced items, even one missed order would be a substan-
tial loss, frequent monitoring is an essential task.)

The job analysis is now complete. What remains is to use the job
analysis results to create the job description, in exercise 5.

Exercise 5. The Security Job Description

Estimated Time: Two Hours
Use the model in Appendix F to write a job description for each job or
job set. Use the results from Exercise 4 to indicate whether or not the
job is security-sensitive, and list the essential functions—those tasks
that are fundamental (as opposed to marginal) to the job position. List
also job tasks of lesser importance and also those that are less frequently
performed.

Notice in Appendix F that some of the job tasks are written using the
terms "knowledge" (performance of the task requires some passive
knowledge about the subject), "skills" (the task requires certain skills,
such as those that have been or can be learned), and "abilities" (the task
requires certain aptitudes, such as mathematical, analytical, or others).
One job task, however, simply requires a "certification," a learned skill
(see the first item under the section "List the knowledge, skills, and abilities identified in the job analysis..."). The point is that there are many
ways to write job task statements; however, the knowledge/skills/abilities
examples shown in Appendix F, because they are broader than simply
stating a specific task, are generally more descriptive.

Notice also the "Work Context" section, which describes the physical
abilities required to perform the job tasks—sitting, standing, reaching, the
use of hands. This section is required to identify jobs that require accommodations. You may also include a section describing the work environment, as this information may be useful for recruiting announcements.

Information contained in the job analysis and the job description,
completed in the exercises in this chapter, will be used in the subsequent
chapters, beginning with Chapter 10, the recruitment of job applicants.

CHAPTER 10

THE PEOPLE FRONT: RECRUITMENT FOR SECURITY

Businesses set the standards of integrity and performance for their own workforce, either intentionally or not. Beginning with recruitment, a company can purposely use scientifically developed procedures to assemble a capable and collegial group of coworkers or can, by default, leave things to chance. The standard for "recruitment for security" eliminates chance. This method develops an applicant pool sufficiently large to increase the probability of attracting applicants who can both perform the job well and secure it.

STANDARD 4. RECRUITMENT FOR SECURITY

Goals: Develop a large applicant pool qualified to (1) perform both general and technical job tasks for a security-related job position (or job set) as well as to (2) secure the personal or business identifying information accessible to the requisite job tasks.

Objectives: Use the team approach, the information contained in the security job description, and a method called "snowballing" to attract a large number of job applicants for a given job set.

Exercise 1. "Snowballing"

Estimated Time per Job Set: Three Hours

In industrial and organizational psychology, the term "snowballing" often is used to describe the incremental aggregating of a large number of studies for use in psychometric meta-analysis. In "recruitment for security," this snowballing technique is used to generate a large list of names of individuals who are likely to have interests compatible with a company's performance *and* security standards, that is, individuals known to have the general and technical competencies required for the vacated or new job position of security and authority. The best place to begin snowballing is with potential rehires—previous employees who voluntarily left for other jobs. The task is, first, to reconsider and then solicit former employees and, second, to seek their referrals of friends and relatives who also might be contacted for current or future job vacancies.

Begin by reviewing the job description for the general and technical requirements essential to performing the job tasks for the job (or job set) under consideration. For this job (and in this exercise), the task is to make a list from personnel records of previous employees who resigned for better jobs.

Go back into and review the records of previous employees to generate a long list of valued employees who were lost to other companies but who might reconsider the vacated or new job position in your company. Personnel records will reveal qualified performers of reputable character. Inform these individuals of the job vacancy first by either telephone calls or e-mail announcements and then, within two weeks, with follow-up letters of invitation to rejoin your company.

When speaking to or corresponding with these former employees, continue to "snowball" the list by asking them for referrals. Research in social psychology shows that people with similar likes, behaviors, and characteristics are attracted to and associate with one another. In the context of workplace characteristics, the friends and relatives of former employees identified as good performers and with reputations of integrity are likely to share those same attributes; and some of those individuals also may possess the technical requirements for the position of security. After the snowballing list has been made with former employees, *next increment this list with referrals from current employees.*

Exercise 2. Involve Current Employees

Estimated Time: Three Hours
Replicate the previous exercise involving former employees with current employees. Increment the snowballing list with names obtained from current employees having personnel records showing high workplace performance and security-related characteristics; that is, those individuals having characteristics that match the general competencies from the job analysis and who are likely to know of relatives, friends, customers, or suppliers with similar characteristics. The "general" competencies, recall, pertain to the requirements for a job; for security-related jobs that have access to or use personal or business identifying information, the "Importance to the Job" section in the job analysis would have identified *job* characteristics such as "trustworthiness," "conscientiousness," or similar others. (Recall also that the job analysis is the basis for all personnel functions, beyond recruitment. The job characteristics, therefore, will resurface in Chapter 11 when conducting the "Personnel Selection for Security" exercises.)

Exercise 3. Solicit New Applicants

Estimated Time: Four Hours
Working from the security job description, create an increasingly larger applicant pool by sending e-mail and written announcements to geographically disbursed newspapers and job counseling centers in vocational schools, community colleges, and universities. Also post this announcement on your e-business Web site. The announcement should specify both "general" and "technical" competencies required by the

job tasks, as identified by the job analysis and summarized in the job description. Increment the applicant pool list with the names of respondents. *Then, for additional names, contact local personnel agencies.*

Exercise 4. Use Personnel Agencies with Caution

Some personnel agencies that provide contract or temporary employees may be reliable sources for the job vacancy. But be cautious. From work with police departments and based on investigations conducted in the Michigan State University Identity Theft Crime Lab, some employees who were contracted through personnel agencies have had ulterior motives and have stolen and fraudulently used coworkers' identities.

Investigations also indicate that some perpetrators obtain contract or temporary employment with a company specifically for the purpose of identity theft. Additionally, research indicates that, relative to permanent employees, temporary employees are less likely to be committed to or satisfied with the job and also often are held to lesser standards of accountability than are the permanent employees. Before using a personnel agency, determine the personnel selection criteria the agency uses to outsource contract or temporary employees. Chapter 11, on personnel selection for security, describes these criteria in detail.

THE PEOPLE FRONT: PERSONNEL SELECTION FOR SECURITY

To compete in the global marketplace, companies require a high-performing workforce. To remain competitive, companies require high internal information security to safeguard their valued assets—the performers and their customers. These goals can be accomplished by selecting job applicants who can perform and who also will comply with a company culture of honesty. The Business Information Security Program (BISP) meets these two objectives using an assessment battery that analyzes the degree of "fit" between an applicant's qualifications and experience and the demand of the job *and also* the extent to which an applicant is likely to help enforce and comply with the security standards.

However, certain conditions must be met. The four selection standards—the four tests that comprise the assessment battery—cannot under the Equal Employment Opportunity Commission (EEOC) guidelines and Title VII be administered to current employees. Current employees perform their jobs well and safeguard the confidentiality of information, or they should not be retained. The purpose of the assessment battery is to lay a foundation in which the job performance and the security of information will be guaranteed for applicants for future employment who are hired into an honest company culture. Using the assessment battery developed in Chapters 11 to 14 for *current* employees would violate provisions under Title VII for the fairness of personnel practices. However, Chapters 15 and 16 *do* affect current employees, because here is where the honest company culture is developed and maintained. The combination of selecting job applicants on the basis of integrity for security into a company culture that also promotes integrity for security, using the methods described in these chapters, are the two key components guaranteed to prevent insider identity theft while also safeguarding the workplace. The integrity test in Chapter 13 will screen out applicants who seek employment for less-than-honorable reasons or who may lack initiative to uphold the company standards for information security.

The battery is a composite of four scientifically developed tests to measure four job-related characteristics: cognitive ability, motivation, integrity, and interpersonal skills. Measures of cognitive ability and motivation are the performance measures that estimate the person-job fit, and the measure of integrity is the security test that estimates the initiative of a job applicant to help protect, enforce, and comply with "work process" security standards, the topic of exercises in Chapter 18. Additionally, the BISP battery includes an interpersonal skills test for businesses recruiting to fill multiple job positions that are either team-based or for positions that require interactions with customers.

Cognitive ability, motivation, integrity, and interpersonal skills are job-related attributes that can be measured with a high degree of accuracy, provided the tests are developed to meet the scientific standards described in each of these next four chapters and which are required by the EEOC guidelines and Title VII statutes for fairness in hiring. These BISP assessment standards—the four tests—meet those legal provisions, and each test is applicable and effective for all businesses and all job sets, regardless of rank or type, provided these jobs fit the "security-sensitive" job analysis classification in Chapter 9.

STANDARD 5. PERSONNEL SELECTION
FOR SECURITY

Goal: Investigate and make recommendations to upper management for two options for a cognitive *ability* test for future personnel selection.

Specific Objectives: A company has two options for obtaining personnel selection assessments (sometimes also called tests or measures). The first option is to use an *existing* test, one developed by a company specializing in personnel selection assessments. The second option is to develop a *company-owned* proprietary test. The cost factors depend on the company (for an existing test) or the specialist (the test developer). In the long term and depending on the number of applicants selected each year, the costs for both can be comparable. The two specific objectives are to investigate both options in terms of costs and test credibility. These two objectives will be the same for selecting each of the four tests—the selection standards. Thus, the *procedures* in Chapters 11 to 14 are identical; only the *type of test* differs.

Orientation

When an existing cognitive ability test is obtained from a test developing company, the purchaser usually is involved in only one part of the personnel selection procedure: the administration of the test to job applicants. The testing company scores the test, interprets the results, provides feedback on recommendations for selection based on these results, and charges a fee for each applicant tested. The test, although administered to many job applicants in many businesses, nonetheless remains consistently effective, because the scoring of the test items remains confidential with the testing company. The option of using an existing test can be useful for small companies with few employees, but it is relatively more costly for larger companies with many and frequent new hires or for companies with large turnover rates, regardless of company size.

The second option is to hire a specialist to develop a company-owned test, which becomes a proprietary asset. For companies that have implemented the standards of the Business Information Security Program, the utility (effectiveness) of a proprietary test will have considerable longevity because this company's information processes, including the test scoring and the rules for interpreting the test results, are highly secured. So, therefore, is the test scoring and the rules for interpreting the test results. Whether a company uses an existing test or develops its own, the BISP project team must consider several factors.

For the first option, selecting an already published cognitive ability test, the team initially must evaluate the test's predictive validity and reliability. Validity means the test measures what it purports to measure—in this case, cognitive ability. Reliability refers to consistency in test results when administered more than one time to the same individual. Regardless of the type or rank of the job, higher cognitive ability translates to greater ability to perform the job tasks. Cognitive ability is, therefore, an important predictor of job performance. Unfortunately, many existing tests on the market today fail to produce the intended results; that is, many off-the-shelf tests fail to exhibit validity, and a test with no evidence for validity is of no value and does not comply with the EEOC guidelines and Title VII statutes on test fairness. The procedure for selecting an existing test must begin with obtaining the test manuals from the test publisher. Most published tests have manuals that describe how the test was developed, how the validity and reliability were established, the standardized method used to administer the test to job applicants, and the costs involved. Sometimes a manual also will recommend a cut score or range of cut scores within which a job applicant would be considered, but this is most often a decision made by the purchasing company.

The test manual of an existing test must document evidence for test fairness.[1] The test must also exhibit a special type of validity, called "predictive validity." Predictive validity of a cognitive ability test is an estimate of how well a job applicant may perform the job tasks. Predictive validities are reported as values that range from 0.0 to 1.0. A cognitive ability test with predictive validity in the .20 to .30 range is considered acceptable, and a test with predictive validity greater than

.30 is considered an excellent predictor of future performance. Reliability estimates are also values ranging from 0.0 to 1.0. Consider a test reliable if the value is .70 or greater. Once the validity and the reliability of a test are established, the next steps are the evaluation of the test administration procedures and the computation of the total costs.

For evaluating the test administration procedures, the test manual should provide instructions for test taking, including the time involved. Some cognitive ability tests are designed to be administered either individually or in groups, using paper-and-pencil formats or computerized software that can be administered on site or online over the Internet. Test-taking times can range from as little as 12 minutes to as much as one hour, and computerized tests can be administered and scored immediately either in-house or from remote locations. Given these many alternatives, cost factors can vary widely.

A well-developed test manual will detail the costs per person, including a breakdown cost that decreases per person as more tests are purchased. The usual costs are for:

1. One copy of the test per job applicant
2. The scoring of each test
3. Interpreting of test results per test
4. The final report

When reviewing this or other manuals that accompany the test, look also for the time frame for completion of the entire process, from the scoring to the receipt of report.

Three good sources for locating test publishers are available. Appendix G lists several reputable test developers known personally by this author for their expertise in test development and validation. The Society for Industrial and Organizational Psychology (SIOP) Web site, *www.siop.com*, provides a list of other specialists. A "specialist" in industrial and organizational psychology has earned a Ph.D. through four or more years of training in test development and validation and applied statistics. In contrast, specialists in clinical or counseling psychology focus on mental health issues; these individuals, who earn either masters' or doctoral degrees, must be licensed to administer tests. To increase their client populations, many clinical psychologists today are moving into the industrial and organizational psychology field. When selecting a *personnel* test, therefore, it is important to distinguish between tests that determine mental health and tests that provide estimates of cognitive ability required to perform job tasks. To search for industrial and organizational Ph.D. specialists on the SIOP Web site, select the radio buttons for both businesses and individuals and use the search term "test development."

A third often overlooked but valuable resource for locating test publishers is the library at a community college or university. The reference sections at most academic libraries carry a series of several large volumes titled the *Mental Measurements Yearbooks*. The yearbooks are continuously updated and include most or all published cognitive ability (and other) tests. For most tests, the yearbook reports the range of predictive validity that can be expected from using the test; the reliability of the test; the cost of the test per person; and the contact (and sometimes additional) information. Eliminate from consideration any test for which there is no documented evidence for validity and reliability.

The descriptions below are based on reviews by K. Geisinger and F.L. Schmidt that were reported in the *Fourteenth Mental Measurements Yearbook*.[2] These illustrate the information the team will need to compare and contrast existing tests. This information also will be useful later on when considering developing a company-owned test.

> *Reviews (Geisinger and Schmidt) from the Mental Measurements Yearbook:*
>
> The Wonderlic Personnel Test (WPT) was designed to be used by businesses to determine "how easily individuals can be trained, how well they can adjust and solve problems on the job, and how well satisfied they are likely to be with the demands of the job." The WPT is "face valid," that is, each test item is an obvious measure of ability. (However, not all tests need be or are intentionally face valid; that is, the items themselves may appear to be unrelated to the name of the test. This test, nonetheless, may exhibit predictive validity, as described the paragraph below.)

The WPT can be administered individually or in groups to adults ages 15 and up.

The cost in 2000 was $1.80 per test. The test is available in Canadian, Swedish, French, Spanish, Tagalog, Vietnamese, German, Chinese, Portuguese, Japanese, Korean, Russian, large print, Braille, and audio editions. The test is composed of 50 multiple-choice or short answer questions that are administered in 12 minutes.

The WPT Manual reports that predictive validity coefficients (values) are provided for job families (job sets), and the validity coefficients range from .22 to .67. (Recall from above that validities in the .20 to .30 range are acceptable and validities greater than .30 are considered high in the personnel context.)

The reliability of the WPT has also been subjected to considerable evaluation.

The WPT Manual reports test-retest reliabilities of .82 to .94 and longitudinal coefficients (values) as high as .94. (Recall that a reliability of .70 or greater is considered acceptable.)

In a section on test fairness, the WPT Manual reports the test has been found to be fair and appropriate for use in employment settings. The test should be administered, scored, and interpreted by someone qualified to analyze intelligence quotients (e.g., a Ph.D.-trained specialist in industrial and organizational psychology).

Considering that the WPT takes only 12 minutes to administer and given the evidence for the test's validity and reliability in employment settings, the WPT is one test the team might obtain for purposes of test comparison.

A final word before moving on: Tests such as those described in these chapters are scientifically developed to be valid and reliable, which means that many of these types of tests must be administered (to job applicants) by experts trained to use the special, standardized procedures required for test administration. Small businesses that do not have a qualified employee on staff can consider employee training as part of the test purchase (option A) or development package (option B). The trained employee then would administer the tests and submit them to the test publisher for scoring, interpretation, and compilation of the final report. A second alternative is to engage an industrial and organizational expert to administer the tests. In any case, do not allow the costs of testing prevent test use in your company: Recall that *people* are the first line of defense for business information security.

Exercise 1. The Cognitive Ability Test: Option A—Obtain, Review, Compare, and Recommend an Existing Test

Estimated Time: Four Hours
Use the team approach to obtain the test manuals for at least three cognitive ability tests from one or more of the three sources—Appendix G, the SIOP Web site, and/or the *Mental Measurements Yearbooks*. Once the manuals are obtained, review and compare the three tests' manuals on these points:

- Documented evidence for "predictive" validity
- Documented evidence for reliability
- Evidence for compliance with EEOC and Title VII guidelines on test fairness
- Description of costs: test administration, interpretation, scoring, results, other
- Description of testing procedures: administration, scoring, interpretation, other
- Description of and rationale for a recommended cutoff score—the lowest acceptable score to be considered for the job
- Test format: paper/pencil, computerized software, Web site administered?
- If computerized or Web site administered: Obtain documented evidence for validity, reliability, and test fairness using these methods.

For each of at least three tests, weigh all of the above factors and then select one test as an option for management consideration for future job applicant testing. Next, consider option B, developing a proprietary test that becomes a company's tangible asset. With this option, the business owns the test items and there are no incremental and ongoing charges by a test publisher because company employees are trained by the specialist to administer, score, interpret, and report the test results. The industrial and organizational specialist collects data and performs a development and validation procedure, establishes strong values for predictive validity and reliability, and conducts statistical analysis to ensure the test meets legal requirements for test fairness.

In exercise 2, the team obtains information on developing a proprietary test, thus enabling it to weigh and recommend to upper management the two options: purchase an existing test or develop one's own.

Exercise 2. The Cognitive Ability Test: Option B—
Develop a Company Proprietary Test

Estimated Time: Four Hours
In this exercise, the team will locate, interview, and compare the test development and validation methods and costs for at least three industrial and organizational specialists. Industrial and organizational psychology is a highly specialized discipline that requires extensive knowledge and training in the development of mathematical algorithms designed to estimate work-related attributes such as cognitive ability, motivation, and other job characteristics. The time and costs for such test development and validation can take up to six months and range from $50,000 to $150,000 or more, depending on the size and complexity of the company and the fee scale of the test specialist. Because of these wide ranges in time and cost, it is necessary to compare and contrast industrial and organziational specialists on their experience and consulting fees.

Therefore, from the Web site for the Society for Industrial and Organizational Psychology, *www.siop.com*, and the list in Appendix G, locate and interview by phone, mail, Internet Webinar (online conference), or in person at least three industrial and organizational test experts. For personal interviews (phone, Webinar, or in person), use the team approach in which all members participate to address these questions:

- What other tests has the test expert developed, and what are the estimates of predictive validity and reliability for these tests?
- What is the testing format: paper and pencil, computerized, on site, online?
- What are the total fees? Obtain a breakdown for individuals versus incremental groups; the development and validation procedure; the production of the test's manuals (for evidence of validation and test fairness and for administering, scoring, and interpreting test results); and the estimated cost the company would incur for producing each test.
- Does the expert's fee include the training of your company's personnel to administer, score, and interpret test results? Does this fee include a training manual?
- What is the time frame for the process—test development and validation, the writing and production of the test and test manuals?

Based on the information from at least three I/O specialists, select one for consideration by management as an alternative to option A, using an existing cognitive ability test.

Cognitive ability, however, is only one aspect of the person and one test in the assessment battery. In Chapter 12, the team will select a measure of motivation to estimate how interested a job applicant may be in performing the assigned job tasks.

THE PEOPLE FRONT: SELECT FOR MOTIVATION

The Uniform Standards of the Business Information Security Program (BISP) emphasize performance to remain competitive and security to protect company assets. The cognitive ability test in Chapter 11 estimated performance by matching an applicant's ability with the requirements of a job. However, ability without the motivation to perform the job tasks is unlikely to lead to very good job performance. Similarly, ability and motivation to perform the job without the initiative to help secure company assets would defeat company objectives. This chapter, therefore, is concerned with motivation, the second assessment in the test battery; Chapter 13 emphasizes integrity for security.

One final note before moving on: Remember the conditions of the BISP assessment battery that prohibits the administration of these tests to current employees; doing so would be in direct violation of strict legal statutes for fairness in personnel practices. As previously mentioned, current employees will be expected to help maintain an honest company culture, topics covered in Chapters 15 and 16.

STANDARD 6. SELECT FOR MOTIVATION

Goal: Investigate and make recommendations to upper management for two options for a test of job-related motivation that will be used for future personnel selection.

Specific Objectives: Consider the two options (from Chapter 11 on personnel selection) for obtaining a test of motivation: (1) use an *existing* test, one developed by a test publishing company, or (2) engage an industrial/organizational specialist to develop a *company-owned* proprietary test. For each option, compare and contrast the validity, reliability, and other criteria listed below. Then choose one test from each option to recommend to management as alternatives to consider for adoption.

Orientation

Many tests on the market today measure job-related characteristics, such as cognitive ability and motivation, as discussed in Chapter 11. Some tests are valid, but many are not. Some tests that are valid may also be misused. A test must be selected based on the results of a job analysis that shows the test attribute is related to performing the job tasks.

An example of one reputable and widely known job-related test is the Achievement via Independence scale, which is one of 21 scales (a word synonymous with "tests") contained in the California Psychological Inventory (CPI).[1] In the context of work-relatedness, this scale measures achievement motivation.

The CPI is also widely known for having perhaps the longest history of research documenting evidence for exceptionally strong values of validity and reliability. The CPI is based on over six decades of research, which means that test users can be confident that the tests measure what they purport to measure — in this case, achievement motivation. The CPI contains one notable scale that detects invalid protocols — responses to test items to fake good responses, fake bad responses, or simply to randomly respond. As with other inventories that also contain multiple scales, some but not all of the CPI tests can be administered independently of the others. Therefore, when reviewing inventories such as the CPI, it is important to clarify with the test publisher that the scale of interest meets the criteria of validity and reliability when administered independently.

The CPI Achievement Motivation scale was developed in 1953 to predict educational achievement motivation and was first named the "Honor Point" scale. However, over the years, the scale was found to predict achievement and motivation in a wide range of occupations that required independent thinking, which is why the scale was later assigned the label "Achievement via Independence." The items on this scale were developed so as to purposely lack face validity, which means that the items do not intend to be representative of the name of the scale. The intention is that test users will be unaware until afterward of the type of test being administered and therefore will be less likely to be influenced to respond in one way or another to the test items.

Research shows that the Motivation scale measures on-the-job achievement independently of measures of cognitive ability. The large body of scientific literature on this 32-item scale shows strong validity ranging from .26 to .46 and reliability as high as .90. This scale, therefore, is a good test of on-the-job motivation. The team task is to view the Achievement Motivation scale and two others and select one for possible use in the BISP's four-test battery.

Exercise 1. The Motivation Test: Option A—Obtain, Review, Compare, and Recommend an Existing Test

Estimated Time: Four Hours
Use the team approach to obtain the test manuals for at least three tests of motivation, including the Achievement Motivation scale of the CPI. Use the three sources described in Chapter 11 — Appendix G, the SIOP Web site, and/or the *Mental Measurements Yearbooks*; for the CPI, contact Consulting Psychologists Press, Inc., *at www.cpp-db.com*. Once the three tests are obtained, then the team as a group is to review and compare the test manuals on each of these criteria:

- Documented evidence for "predictive" validity
- Documented evidence for reliability
- Evidence for compliance with EEOC and Title VII guidelines on test fairness
- Description of costs: test administration, interpretation, scoring, results, other
- Description of testing procedures: administration, scoring, interpretation, other
- Description of and rationale for a recommended cutoff score — the lowest acceptable score to be considered for the job
- Test format: paper/pencil, computerized software, Web site administered?
- If computerized or Web site administered: Obtain documented evidence for validity, reliability, and test fairness using these methods.

For the CPI Achievement Motivation Scale:

- Obtain documented evidence on all the items just listed for using the scale independently of the other CPI scales.
- Obtain documented evidence that items of the Invalid Protocol scale can also be used with the Achievement Motivation scale, independent of the remaining CPI scales.

For each of the three tests, carefully weigh all of the above factors. Then select one test to recommend that management include as the test of motivation for the BISP battery. Management may, however, prefer owning the test. Next, therefore, consider option B, in which an I/O specialist develops a test that would become the proprietary property of the company.

Exercise 2. The Motivation Test: Option B— Develop a Company Proprietary Test

Estimated Time: Four Hours
Continue with the team approach by assigning team pairs to locate and obtain at least three I/O specialists for an interview with each, conducted by all of the team members (i.e., a "group" interview). Compare and contrast

the test development and validation methods and consulting fees of these three specialists. Again, use either or both the Society for Industrial and Organizational Psychology Web site at *www.siop.com* and the list in Appendix G to locate an I/O specialist.

Once identified, interview (by phone, Webinar, mail, or in person) each of the experts to determine their qualifications for developing a test of motivation that can be administered independently of other tests. Be sure to cover these questions:

- What other tests has the I/O expert developed, and what are the estimates of predictive validity and reliability for these tests?
- What is the testing format: paper and pencil, computerized, on site, online?
- What are the total fees? Obtain a breakdown for individuals versus incremental groups; the development and validation procedure; the production of the test's manuals (for evidence of validation and test fairness and for administering, scoring, interpreting test results); and the estimated cost the company would incur for producing each test.
- Does the expert's consulting fee include the training of company personnel to administer, score, and interpret test results?
- Does the consulting fee include a training manual?
- Can the I/O specialist develop a motivation test for which results will be unrelated to cognitive ability, integrity, or interpersonal skills?
- What is the time frame for the process: test development and validation, writing and producing the test and test manuals, and training employees?

Based on comparisons of the experts' responses and documented supporting evidence for these questions, select one specialist whom management might consider to develop a company-owned motivation test as an alternative to using a publisher-owned, nonproprietary test.

Be sure to check off the exercises as completed (Appendix A). Then move on to Chapter 13, selecting for integrity and security.

CHAPTER 13

THE PEOPLE FRONT: SELECT FOR INTEGRITY AND SECURITY

Contrary to common thought, most identities are stolen from businesses; fewer are stolen from garbage Dumpsters or by online hackers. Phishing, the fraudulent cloning of a legitimate business's Web site or sending a fake e-mail letter requesting personal information under the auspices of updating company records, is becoming increasingly known because of the large numbers of identities that are reported stolen in a single phishing attack. But although thefts do occur from these sources, as well as from homes, cars, and persons, the majority of identity thefts are committed inside the workplace by a relatively few dishonest employees who steal the personal identification data of a company's most valued assets: customers and coworkers.

Oftentimes perpetrators will hire into a company on a contract basis for temporary employment. Some insiders with borderline criminal minds are used as pawns by outsider criminal friends to obtain access to company information, such as names, addresses, and Social Security numbers of employees or customers. Although they may not themselves use the stolen identities of their coworkers or customers, these indirectly involved employees are, nonetheless, insider criminals because they directly facilitate the credit card, bank fraud, and other crimes committed using the stolen identities.

The solutions are three:

1. Businesses can incorporate into the personnel selection system a scientifically developed test to select new job applicants for characteristics of integrity and honesty.
2. Company cultures of honesty can be developed and easily maintained by their vast majority of hardworking and honest employees who need to feel safe where they spend a great part of their lives.
3. The foregoing solutions to secure business borders can be made possible only by progressive companies whose upper-level management proactively supports such initiatives.

This chapter addresses the first solution: selecting for integrity and honesty. It must be reemphasized, however, that a test of integrity and honesty cannot, under the Equal Employment Opportunity Commission (EEOC) guidelines and Title VII, be administered to current employees. These employees were selected into their job positions using other personnel practices, and the use of this or other tests in the battery for current employees is in direct violation of strict legal statutes.

STANDARD 7. SELECT FOR INTEGRITY AND SECURITY

Goal: Investigate and make recommendations to upper management for two options for a test of job-related integrity for security, which will be used for future personnel selection.

Specific Objectives: Consider two options for obtaining a test of integrity for security: (1) use an *existing* test (one developed by test publishing company), or (2) engage an industrial and organizational (I/O) specialist to develop a *company-owned* proprietary test. For each option, compare and contrast the validity, reliability, and other criteria as in Chapter 12 and, for convenience, listed again below. Then choose one test from each of the two options to recommend to management as alternative considerations for adoption.

Orientation

Insider theft is not a new phenomenon: Criminals operate wherever they can, be it on the street or in the workplace. In past decades, one of the greatest losses companies had to absorb was the cost of shrinkage due to the theft of merchandise by dishonest employees and other shoplifters. And, since the early 1950s, white-collar crimes of insider fraud and embezzlement have become so prevalent that entire academic disciplines have grown around the topic and any number of books and articles continue to be published on these crimes and their devastating effects on society.

Today, in the information era, in addition to shrinkage, fraud, and embezzlement, criminal insiders steal information—personal and business identities. And when it comes to the insider theft of identities, not only are the customers at risk but so are the coworkers of the insider criminal. Unlike insider shrinkage, fraud, and embezzlement, however, there is no way that companies can absorb the sometimes devastating psychological costs to employees or customers whose identities have been stolen and used to commit identity crimes. Companies have become more compassionate about giving employees time off work to recover from identity thefts and, from the increasing numbers of requests to the Michigan State University Business Partnerships in Prevention, it is apparent that companies also are establishing advocacy services to help victims in their recoveries.

These efforts, though laudable, are merely reactive and do nothing to prevent the identity thefts in the first place. By incorporating into personnel selection practices integrity tests for security, insider thefts largely can be prevented. Volumes of applied research conducted over many years in business settings have shown without any doubt that scientifically developed tests that comply with EEOC and Title VII guidelines are capable of detecting antisocial and criminal behavior in the workplace.

Why do all businesses not use these tests uniformly? There are seven reasons.

1. Many managers are unaware that such tests exist.

2. Many managers who are aware of these tests have no confidence in them; that is, lacking knowledge in the area of scientific testing, managers have no basis to believe these tests are effective.

3. Some of those managers who *do* recognize the value of using integrity for security tests purchase the tests from unknown companies; off-the-shelf tests often lack in validity and reliability and, therefore, do not work.

4. Other managers erroneously believe that integrity for security tests are cost prohibitive, an incorrect assumption, as this chapter reveals.

5. Some managers, although they know the tests are effective, are fearful of using them for legal reasons based on publicity given companies that have used the tests incorrectly, that is, without evidence that the characteristics being measured are job-related. Without having conducted a job analysis, companies are unable to distinguish between job positions that are and are not security-related.

6. Other managers mistakenly equate integrity for security tests with background checks: Background checks, like polygraph tests, are not specifically related to the tasks of the job, and these tests lack evidence for validity and reliability—the EEOC requirements. For these reasons, background checks and polygraph tests are generally illegal for purposes of personnel selection, except for specialized and federal government positions. In contrast, scientifically developed integrity tests for security, when based on the results of a job analysis, do conform to the legal statutes.

7. Not only the managers, but some employees as well, have preconceived ideas that, for example, if integrity tests are administered to job applicants, then the broad assumption must be that all employees are delinquent. Of course, this notion cannot be farther from the truth. But facts must be faced: Criminals are everywhere, including where people work. These perpetrators,

like the proverbial bad apple in a barrel, spread rot to everyone. And criminals do not discriminate when it comes to crime: They will steal *anyone's* identity—customers and employees alike.

The picture need not be all that bleak, however, because identity thefts by these relatively few dishonest employees can be stopped. How? In three simple and inexpensive ways:

1. Companies can use personnel selection tests for job positions of security to select for integrity and honesty.
2. Companies can create organizational cultures in which shrinkage, fraud, embezzlement, and other workplace crimes, including identity thefts, are openly acknowledged and addressed as potential and largely preventable company assaults.
3. Upper-level management can progressively and proactively support the majority of hardworking and honest employees who can help to maintain an honest company culture in which they can feel secure.

Ironically, it is the employees' identities that often are stolen from companies, and it is also employees who can make the difference when it comes to preventing identity thefts. Ultimately, therefore, the people who make and maintain the company are the first line of defense against identity theft—and these individuals are company employees and their customers.

To address the first solution, one of the most reputable tests of integrity for security is the Socialization scale of the California Psychological Inventory (CPI).[1] The Socialization scale can be administered independently of the other CPI scales; results from administering this test are valid and reliable; and, when based on a security job analysis (Chapter 9), the use of the test by a company meets the guidelines set forth by the EEOC under Title VII.

This integrity test for security was labeled Socialization by the test developer, Dr. Harrison Gough, because the scale was developed based on the theory that early socialization in the family, at school, and with peers would later in life predict delinquent or criminal behavior.

This socialization theory has been tested and verified in over 1,000 studies. The strength of the Socialization scale became so well known among researchers and test developers that the scale is the forerunner of most, if not all, other honesty and integrity tests published today. In fact, the items in most tests published in the United States were borrowed in part or in whole from the Socialization scale, sometimes verbatim. Today, the Socialization scale ranks among the most effective integrity test for security on the market. The validity is in the .50 to .70 range, and the reliability approximates .90—extremely strong values that indicate the utility of this scale for selection purposes where the goal is to select for integrity for security.

There are a number of other reputable tests as well, and costs vary among them. Therefore, to select a test that meets company needs and budgets, it is important to investigate several.

Exercise 1. The Integrity for Security Test: Option A—Obtain, Review, Compare, and Recommend an Existing Test

Estimated Time: Four Hours

Use the team approach to obtain the test manuals for at least three tests of integrity for security, including the Socialization scale of the CPI. Use the three sources described in Chapters 11 and 12—Appendix G, the SIOP Web site, and/or the *Mental Measurements Yearbooks*. For the CPI, the test publisher and Web site address is Consulting Psychologists Press, Inc., at *www.cpp-db.com*. Once obtained, compare (either in team pairs or as a group) the test manuals on these criteria:

- Documented evidence for "predictive" validity
- Documented evidence for reliability
- Evidence for compliance with EEOC and Title VII guidelines on test fairness
- Description of costs: test administration, interpretation, scoring, results, other

- Description of testing procedures: administration, scoring, interpretation, other
- Description of and rationale for a recommended cutoff score—the lowest acceptable score to be considered for the job
- Test format: paper/pencil, computerized software, Web site administered?
- If computerized or Web site administered: Obtain documented evidence for validity, reliability, and test fairness using these methods.

For the CPI Socialization scale:

- Establish whether or not the Invalid Protocol scale also can be used with the Socialization scale, to detect false responding to the scale's items.

After carefully weighing each of the above factors, select one test to recommend to management as a standard for the Business Information Security Program's assessment battery. Because some companies prefer to invest in such tests as tangible assets, exercise 2 provides that alternative.

Exercise 2. The Integrity for Security Test: Option B—Develop a Company Proprietary Test

Estimated Time: Four Hours
Using team "pairs," locate and obtain the names of at least three I/O specialists for an interview. The purpose is to obtain information on the following points so as to compare and contrast these experts' methods of test development and validation and their respective consulting costs. As before, use one or both of the following resources to locate an I/O specialist: the Society for Industrial and Organizational Psychology Web site at *www.siop.com* and/or the list in Appendix G. Once identified, conduct a team interview (by phone, Webinar, or in person) with each of three experts to determine their qualifications, based on these criteria:

- What tests has the I/O expert developed, and what are the estimates of predictive validity and reliability for these tests?

- What testing formats does the I/O expert develop: paper and pencil, computerized, on site, online?
- What are the total consulting fees for developing such a test? Obtain a breakdown for individuals versus group costs; the development and validation procedure; the production of the test's manuals (for evidence of validation and test fairness and for administering, scoring, interpreting test results); and the estimated cost the expert would incur for producing each test.
- Does the consulting fee include the training of company personnel to administer, score, and interpret test results?
- Does the consulting fee include a training manual?
- Can the I/O specialist develop an integrity test for security for which results will be unrelated to cognitive ability or interpersonal skills?
- What is the time frame for test development and validation, the writing and production of the test and test manuals, and the training of employees?

Based on comparisons of three experts' responses and their documented supporting evidence for these questions, select one specialist to give management the choice of either purchasing a publisher-owned test or developing one that becomes company property.

To summarize thus far: The Business Information Security Program requires a series of standards to help secure the people front. These people standards are directed toward both performance and security, and they begin with a personnel selection system that includes tests of cognitive ability, motivation, and integrity. In addition, a measure of interpersonal skills, which is the last test (Chapter 14) in the BISP assessment battery, is for businesses in which employees interact with one another or with customers in the process of performing job tasks.

THE PEOPLE FRONT: SELECT FOR INTERPERSONAL SKILLS

For efficiency and cost-savings utility, and to remain competitive in an information-based economy, the standards of the Business Information Security Program (BISP) incorporate information security into traditional personnel functions that companies already may have in place. One traditional personnel selection practice that can be expected to increase in a service-based economy is the use of tests of interpersonal skills, which is why this test is included as the fourth standard of the BISP assessment battery.

A test of interpersonal skills can help to determine the fit or match between a job and the job applicant or the level of training needed by an applicant to perform that job's interactive tasks. The use of a test of interpersonal skills, as with all other personnel selection tests, must be based on the results of the job analysis, as not all jobs require interpersonal interactions.

Today, however, many jobs that require confidentiality of information also involve customer service in which employees interpersonally interact with their customers or consumers—a company's potential customers.

Whether these employee-customer interactions occur face-to-face, over the telephone or the Internet, or in written communication, their outcomes directly impact the reputation, performance, and security of corporate information. Similarly, many other jobs, such as support positions, although they may not directly involve customer service, require teamwork, such as in the development of these BISP standards. Other jobs, such as some entry-level positions that involve data entry and basic accounting or clerical tasks, may involve little or no interpersonal interactions to perform the job tasks but are, nonetheless, positions of security because of access to customer or coworker identities. Thus, although not all companies may require a test of interpersonal skills for job applicants, for jobs where tasks do involve an interpersonal component, this test is a required BISP standard. One last reminder: Under the Equal Employment Opportunity Commission (EEOC) guidelines and Title VII, this test cannot be administered to *current* employees.

STANDARD 8. SELECT FOR INTERPERSONAL SKILLS

Goal: Investigate and make recommendations to upper management for two options for a test of job-related interpersonal skills, which will be used for future personnel selection.

Specific Objectives: Consider the two options for obtaining a test of interpersonal skills: (1) use an *existing* test, one developed by test publishing company, or (2) engage an industrial and organizational (I/O) specialist to develop a *company-owned* proprietary test. For each option, compare and contrast the validity, reliability, and other criteria listed, then choose one test from each of the two options to recommend to management as alternative considerations for future personnel selection practices.

Orientation

The validity and reliability of the scales of the California Psychological Inventory have been established in hundreds of studies over the years and are used today by hundreds of companies for personnel selection practices, which is why this chapter, once again, uses an example from that inventory. The test of interpersonal skills is formally titled the Sociability scale. The test manual provides a lengthy list of applied research in businesses showing that the Sociability scale measures the ability to be cooperative and effective when dealing with others.

The test manual also reports one interesting validation study conducted in 1992 at an international communications company that followed the progress of 229 persons hired in a managerial development program. The Sociability scale had been administered at the time of hiring, and purpose of the study was to determine the effect of Sociability on promotion or nonpromotion to middle management seven or more years later. The results showed a validity of .30 and reliability in the .90 range, indicating that higher scores on Sociability were also strongly related to job promotions. In addition to this study on management tracks, the validity of the Sociability scale has been tested on a wide range of other job positions in many occupations. The Sociability scale is but one example, however, of dozens of reputable tests of interpersonal skills that the BISP team might consider in the following exercises.

Exercise 1. The Test of Interpersonal Skills: Option A—Obtain, Review, Compare, and Recommend an Existing Test

Estimated Time: Four Hours
Use the team approach to obtain the test manuals for at least three tests of interpersonal skills, including the Sociability scale of the CPI. Use the three sources described in Chapters 11 to 13—Appendix G, the Society for Industrial and Organizational Psychology (SIOP) Web site, and/or the *Mental Measurements Yearbooks*. For the CPI, the test publisher and Web site address is Consulting Psychologists Press, Inc., at *www.cpp-db.com*. Once obtained, compare (either in team pairs or as a group) the test manuals on the usual criteria:

- Documented evidence for "predictive" validity
- Documented evidence for reliability

- Evidence for compliance with EEOC and Title VII guidelines on test fairness
- Description of costs: test administration, interpretation, scoring, results, other
- Description of testing procedures: administration, scoring, interpretation, other
- Description of and rationale for a recommended cutoff score—the lowest acceptable score to be considered for the job
- Test format: paper/pencil, computerized software, Web site administered?
- If computerized or Web site administered: Obtain documented evidence for validity, reliability, and test fairness using these methods.

For the CPI Sociability scale:

- Establish whether the Invalid Protocol scale can also be used with the Sociability scale to detect false responding to the scale's items.
- Also establish whether validity evidence exists to use the Sociability scale as a stand-alone scale or whether the scale must be used in conjunction with other CPI scales.

Weigh each of the preceding factors, then select one test to recommend to management as the fourth standard for BISP's assessment battery. Now consider exercise 2, to determine the utility of investing in a company-owned test.

Exercise 2. The Test of Interpersonal Skills: Option B— Develop a Company Proprietary Test

Estimated Time: Four Hours

Using the team pair model (divide duties and work in pairs) to locate and obtain the names of at least three I/O specialists for an interview. As in the previous *people* chapters, obtain information on the points below so as to compare and contrast the experts on their methods of test development and validation and the consulting costs for each. Again, locate an I/O specialist using the Society for Industrial and Organizational Psychology Web site *www.siop.com* and/or the list in Appendix G. Once so identified, determine the experts' qualifications in a team interview conducted by phone, Webinar, or in person, using these criteria:

- What tests has the I/O expert developed, and what are the estimates of predictive validity and reliability for these tests?
- What testing formats does the I/O expert develop: paper and pencil, computerized, on site, online?
- What are the total consulting fees for developing such a test? Obtain a breakdown for individuals versus group costs; the development and validation procedure; the production of the test's manuals (for evidence of validation and test fairness and for administering, scoring, interpreting test results); and the estimated cost the expert would charge for producing each test.
- Does the consulting fee include the training of company personnel to administer, score, and interpret test results?
- Does the consulting fee include a training manual?
- Can the I/O specialist develop an interpersonal skills test for which the test results will be unrelated to cognitive ability, motivation, and integrity?
- What is the time frame for test development and validation, the writing and production of the test and test manuals, and the training of employees?

Based on comparisons of the experts' responses and also on supporting evidence for these questions, select one specialist for management to consider as an option to using an existing test.

With this fourth test, the BISP assessment battery is complete. Using the tests in this battery, job applicants will be matched to jobs compatible with their ability and skills: cognitive ability, motivation, and interpersonal skills. The use of these standards guarantees a close person-job fit for new applicants, which is the primary determining factor underlying quality job performance. Moreover, the integrity test provides the first line of defense in guaranteeing the security of customer and coworker personal information. The standards collectively ensure both high job performance as well as information security, beginning with the job analysis requirement. These standards are the foundation of the Business Information Security Program.

Reminder: Are you checking off the completed exercises (Appendix A)?

CHAPTER 15

THE PEOPLE FRONT: SOCIALIZATION, COMPANY CULTURE, AND THE REALISTIC JOB PREVIEW

Beginning with the first day on the job and continuing through a process called "organizational socialization," employees learn the ethics of the company culture—its rules, procedures, policies, and formal and informal expectations: what is *said* to be expected and what *is* actually acceptable, based on other employees' behaviors. The company culture is the tabula rasa—the blank slate upon which all that follows depends. For information security, an honest company culture is vital. Standard 9 prepares this backdrop for first impressions of your company's culture of security.

STANDARD 9. COMPANY CULTURE AND THE REALISTIC JOB PREVIEW

Goals: Evaluate, investigate, document, and modify (if necessary) your company's honest company culture.

Specific Objectives: The four exercises in this chapter are progressive building blocks. They are, in ascending order:

1. Assess the current company culture.
2. Further analyze to identify improvements.
3. Use the results from (1) and (2) to develop a "realistic job preview" document.
4. Develop short- and long-term strategic plans to implement policies for an honest company culture.

Of these four objectives, the realistic job preview is the standard that carries forth the company's policies for identity confidentiality. The *traditional* realistic job preview is simply a discussion, preempting false impressions of what is and what is not acceptable. However, when adapted as a security standard, the realistic job preview incorporates into the discussion security and the consequences of security standards violations.

In addition, the realistic job preview is a tangible document that not only describes the job's positive and negative characteristics, but also describes the company's honest culture and specific expectations for maintaining that culture. This document, when first discussed with job applicants and referred to in the same detail later in a job orientation after hire, will leave no doubt as to company rules and coworker expectations for integrity for security.

Orientation

The socialization of a new employee to what is and what is not acceptable by the company's standards starts much earlier than the first day on the job; it begins with the "job preview" on the applicant's first contact with the company representative. An initial contact is the primacy point at which time an individual is most impressionable, and it is a critical stage in the selection process when a company first shows its face validity to an outsider. First impressions matter, and it is at this precise time that a company can either manage or leave to chance a job applicant's perception of the company's culture.

As the exercises in this chapter will reveal, it takes little time, effort, or cost to inform job candidates that the coworkers in this company expect, enforce, and maintain information security. With this forewarning, conveyed by company representatives through a professionally developed realistic job preview, identity theft perpetrators seeking to hire into a company as either temporary or permanent employees are put on notice that this company is on the alert for violations of its ethical standards.

After the realistic job preview, the company's desired culture is reinforced through the types of tests used to determine the applicant-job fit. For example, when a company uses the Sociability and Socialization scales as part of the selection process, the values the company portrays are interpersonal compatibility among coworkers and honesty. These values, reflected in the realistic job preview and reinforced through the assessment battery developed in previous chapters, exemplify how these standards are interdependent and work in combination to secure the business borders from identity thefts.

Exercise 1. Assess the Company Culture

Estimated Time: Three Hours
What is your company's culture? The answer to this question is the first step in creating a company environment that safeguards the confidential information of its employees and customers. To begin this process, use the team approach and the quality-to-security brainstorming method to identify the positive and any negative aspects of the company's culture. The goal is to identify both ethical and unethical policies or procedures, formal or informal, which would color perceptions of the work culture, in terms of security.

Before beginning step 1, review together the structured, step-by-step instructions in Appendix C for brainstorming so as to closely follow the formal procedures. Use the proper seating arrangement and the flip chart with the following task statement.

Step 1. Task Statement 1—*List the procedures and policies of this company that either directly or indirectly reflect the ethical values of honesty and integrity in the workplace.* The points generated from this task statement will be included in the realistic job preview document. As a way to trigger ideas during the personal thinking time and the round robin, consider the *informal* work environment as it is now and the existing *formal* (written) rules and regulations. When finished, post this chart on a nearby wall for ease in reference when conducting exercise 2. Next, conduct brainstorming for the following task statement.

Step 2. Task Statement 2—*List the procedures and policies of this company that either directly or indirectly promote unethical values of honesty and integrity in the workplace.* Indirect practices could simply be policies that fail to promote ethical values. For example, an item on the unethical brainstorming list may be "no recognition," meaning that no recognition is given employees who take precautions to secure confidential business information. When no formal policies recognize or reward positive work practices, the assumption is that these practices are unimportant, that is, not part of the company's culture.

To help trigger ideas, think about how the informal work environment is now and consider any formal or informal rules or regulations that might discourage honesty in the workplace or conscientious attention to security details. When the exercise is completed, post the chart on the wall next to the ethical chart. Both will be used to conduct the following cause-and-effect analysis.

Exercise 2. Further Analyze to Identify Improvements

Estimated Time: Three Hours
Recall that the Business Information Security Program (BISP) is designed so that each succeeding chapter builds on the previous chapter's results and that, within chapters, the exercises also build on one another. Recall also that cause-and-effect analysis is a way to organize ideas generated in brainstorming. Problems that can be visualized according to some

structured guideline and framework (e.g., cause-and-effect analysis fishbone with its four M's used in Chapter 8) help facilitate group discussions to identify resolutions. In exercise 2, therefore, conduct cause-and-effect analysis on the ideas generated in exercise 1. Before beginning, review the step-by-step instructions in Appendix D for conducting cause-and-effect analysis and also the fishbone frameworks displayed in Exhibits D.1 and D.2.

The goals are to eliminate the unethical and to elaborate on the ethical policies and procedures that influence the work environment. Unethical factors may simply be the lack of policies that *fail to promote* ethics in the workplace. Use a flip chart with the quality-to-security management fishbone framework and the four factors thought to underlie all work-related problems: manpower, method, machine, or material.

Step 1. Examine the Unethical List. Write this problem statement on the flip chart, with a fishbone arrowhead pointing to it: "Factors That May Influence Unethical Company Cultures." Through group discussion and decision, list each item on the unethical list under one of the four causes of business problems: manpower, method, machine, or material. For example, the "no recognition" item could be categorized either as "manpower" or "method," where a method could be a policy or procedure.

Next, through group discussion, eliminate each unethical item by generating an opposing alternative policy, procedure, or practice. Referring again to the "no recognition" item on the list, the alternative would be to formally recognize honesty in the workplace through a routinely conducted *organizational* performance evaluation. (Chapter 17 distinguishes between a *personal* and an *organizational* evaluation.) The terms "honesty" and "security" would have been identified in the job analysis for positions that require security, and remember that the Equal Employment Opportunity Commission guidelines pertain to all personnel practices, including performance evaluations.

Replace the unethical opposing items with ethical alternatives under the appropriate category (one of the four M's) on a new fishbone chart, which will be incremented in step 2 with items from the ethical list. Use the following problem statement for this new flip chart: "Incremental Ways to Reflect the Honest Company Culture."

Step 2. Now add to the Ethical List (from step 1). On the flip chart titled "Incremental Ways to Reflect the Honest Company Culture," transfer each item on the list developed in the ethical brainstorming session to one of the four-factor categories: manpower, method, machine, or material. The following realistic job preview will be created using these items.

Exercise 3. Create the Realistic Job Preview

Estimated Time: Four Hours

The team task is to use the lists of items generated in the previous exercises in this chapter to create the text for a realistic job preview document to present to future applicants, detailing among other things company expectations for enforcing and maintaining the security of personal identifying information.

Research on employee turnover shows that employees who are given a realistic preview of the job remain with the company longer. New employees are not surprised when first encountering negative job aspects because the company has not hidden these features but, instead, conscientiously exposed them through a realistic job preview. However, a job preview, if informal, is left to chance interpretations; a formal job preview, presented using descriptive brochures or other documents, clearly informs applicants of company expectations.

This formal job preview document, because it is adapted from the traditional method that focuses only on job performance (and not security), must include the positive and negative features of a job. Because the job specific information will differ depending on the job position, these positive versus negative features can be included as a separate document appended or inserted into the formal job preview document.

This exercise focuses on the incremental list of ethical practices and policies. The goal now is to organize this material into well-written text for a brochure or other document that will become an essential formal company policy for security standards in the workplace.

Exercise 4. Develop the Strategic Plan

Estimated Time: Two–Three Hours

Before making recommendations to management for adopting the improvements in company culture as defined by the realistic job preview (created in the previous exercise 3), develop short- and long-term strategic plans, including specific target dates, for implementing these suggestions. Budgeting may be required to implement some of the items on the ethical list of recommendations and also to format and print the realistic job preview brochure or other document, depending on its design.

The costs involved for developing each standard, over and above the time of the team, can vary, depending on a company's prerogatives. Budgeting aside, the implementation of these results requires setting specific target dates. For example, if honesty in the workplace is to be incorporated into an organization performance evaluation, then specific dates must be established to conduct routine performance evaluations. Appendix H shows an example of one company's strategic time plan.

Now use the information generated in this chapter's exercises to develop and initiate the Security Orientation Program, described next in Chapter 16.

THE PEOPLE FRONT: SOCIALIZING NEWCOMERS TO THE HONEST COMPANY CULTURE

In Chapter 15, the team designed a job preview document that emphasized honesty and integrity and the company's requirement for information security. In this chapter, the team uses the job preview document together with incremental information for a Security Orientation Program that will reinforce what applicants learn in first contacts and to further introduce new employees to your company's security standards.

STANDARD 10. THE SECURITY ORIENTATION PROGRAM

Goals: Create measurable actions to promote honesty and security in the workplace and create an agenda for a two-hour Security Orientation Program.

Specific Objectives: Elaborate on the information in the job preview document for use in an orientation program to socialize new employees to your company's desired culture and its emphasis on the protection of business, customer, and employee identities. Include in this exercise as many current employees as possible: after developing the program, administer it to other employees for feedback and potential modifications.

Orientation

Socialization to an organization begins with the first contact between an interested individual and a company representative. This first contact may be made formally through the company's recruiter or by another company stakeholder, such as an employee, contractor, or supplier. If made through the company recruiter, the first contact would introduce the potential job applicant to the company's desired culture through the formal job preview. However, many first contacts are not made through recruiters; instead, individuals learn about jobs through current employees, friends, relatives, or others. Regardless of the type of initial contact, formal or informal, the potential applicant begins to form an impression of the company, and this socialization continues, also formally or informally, after he or she is hired into the company.

When socialization is informal, a new job incumbent learns from supervisors and other employees what is and what is not accepted. Informal information can be noninclusive, incorrect, and inconsistent with company policies. In such cases, security-related decisions are likely to be based on past work experiences and not on your company's Standards. Companies that develop formal orientation programs do not leave socialization to chance.

Formal socialization is a defined and structured personnel function used to positively influence work behavior. The work behaviors of particular interest, in addition to job performance, are those that will help safeguard confidential information, which is why the Business Information Security Program (BISP) requires as a standard the Security Orientation Program.

Exercise 1. Design the Security Orientation Program

Estimated Time: Four Hours

Exercise 1 in this chapter, unlike previous chapters, first employs brainstorming to generate ideas for each of the four M's—manpower, method, machines, and materials. Then it categorizes each of these ideas using the fishbone framework (used in previous chapters) for generating further discussion and to trigger additional ideas. Before beginning this exercise, review the step-by-step instructions on formal brainstorming (Appendix C) and cause-and-effect analysis (Appendix D).

Step 1. *Develop Measurable Actions.* As a team, conduct brainstorming on each of the four M's (manpower, method, machines, and material) in four separate hour-long brainstorming sessions. For each M, generate a list of measurable actions in which honesty can become an integral part of the company's culture. In step 2, these actions will form the basis of the written agenda for the Security Orientation Program (and in Chapter 17, they will become part of the organizational performance review). Use the following task statement for the brainstorming flip chart, inserting the appropriate M for each session: "Measurable (e.g., manpower) actions that promote honesty in the workplace."

From workshop experiences, ideas for measurable actions for manpower and method are the easiest to generate, although the most action-oriented and often creative ideas come from brainstorming on the other two M's—machines and materials.

For example, machine actions that would help to promote both honesty and security might be rules that: prohibit employees from using other employees' computers, require computer screens be secured from observation by passersby, and ordain similar security precautions for copy, fax, and other equipment. For materials, a measurable action to promote honesty and security might require special handling or routing of security-related documents, such as applications for credit or loans or documents containing employee health or other benefit information.

When brainstorming, try to envision an *ideal* culture that holds sacred proprietary information. For the measurable actions, consider measurable job behaviors that can be rewarded for protecting the theft of personal information.

Step 2. *Organize and Match Measurable Actions* (i.e., job behaviors) with job preview criteria. That is, first use the fishbone framework to organize the measurable actions for each of the four M's. The task statement for the flip chart arrowhead is: "Measurable Actions for Honesty and Security." Next, review the job preview document (Chapter 15) for its security-required policies, procedures, and practices. Through group discussion, assign each criterion—a policy, procedure, or practice—to one of the four M's *in the form of a measurable action.*

Exercise 2. Prepare a Written Agenda for the Security Orientation Program

Estimated Time: Three Hours
Using the measurable actions from exercise 1, create an agenda for a two-hour Security Orientation Program that describes and illustrates "the way things are done around here." This agenda will be followed in exercise 3, when presenting the program to current employees for their feedback and suggestions.

Orientation programs come in many sizes and shapes and can include elaborate videos and expensively bound handbooks that oftentimes go unread. Consider for the present program a simple design that nonetheless must be formally presented. For example, a very effective agenda is one that from time to time involves and alternates different groups of employees, utilizing an inexpensive and easy-to-create PowerPoint presentation that clearly describes to new hires the many measurable actions employees perform to help to promote your company's honest work environment.

Interspersed within the presentation may be one or more brief panel discussions in which three or four employees describe how they perform specific measurable actions that safeguard personal and business identities and thereby promote security in the workplace. Include in the orientation a review of the handout—the Realistic Job Preview document. The sample agenda is shown in Exhibit 16.1.

EXHIBIT 16.1 *The Security Orientation Program of the Information Security Research Institute*

- Introduction to Identity Theft: Safeguarding Business, Customer, and Employee Identities
- Federal Statutes Requiring Standards for Information Security: A Brief Overview
- Measurable Actions: A Description of This Company's Standards for Honesty and Security
- Employee Panel Discussion: "How We Perform Measurable Actions to Protect Information"
- Concluding Statements: "The Way Things Are Done Around Here"

Exercise 3. Present the Security Orientation Program to Current Employees

Estimated Time: Three–Four Hours

Current employees *informally* socialize new employees during day-to-day interactions, but by involving current employees in the development of an orientation program, even that aspect of socialization becomes formalized. Current employees, from their on-the-job experiences, may also have ideas that would contribute to the Security Orientation Program. Further, applied research in organizations shows that employees involved in a process tend to take responsibility for the outcomes, which is why these employees also tend to promote and perpetuate the practices or policies they propose. For all of these reasons, it is important to include as many employees as possible in company initiatives, including the development of the Security Orientation Program.

Therefore, prior to inaugurating this Standard:

1. Present the program to current employees, soliciting their suggestions for possible modifications.
2. Make feasible changes.

3. After approval from upper management and using in-house memos, distribute to all employees a brief outline of the revised Security Orientation Program.

When presenting the program to current employees, include in the agenda a last bullet point for discussion. During this discussion, participants can ask questions to clarify points and make contributions. Also ask employees for *written*, anonymous comments and suggestions.

The Security Orientation Program alone will make no difference in an organization's culture, nor will any of the preceding exercises in isolation. Taken altogether, however, each building block chapter reinforces the objectives for protecting the company's most valued assets through standards that also comply with federal laws requiring information security. The next equally important standard is the appraisal, feedback, and reward system.

CHAPTER 17

THE PEOPLE FRONT: APPRAISAL AND FEEDBACK FOR PERFORMANCE AND SECURITY

On-the-job performance is always appraised, either informally through observation or formally as part of regularly scheduled reviews. Informal appraisals are subjective impressions and do not meet federal laws for fairness in personnel practices; informal appraisals, therefore, may be error prone, and so may any personnel decisions made using such appraisals. Employees deserve to be appraised using formal systems that measure the performance of job competencies identified in the job analysis and nothing more.

The Business Information Security Program (BISP) Standard for appraisal is an all-inclusive, formal *organizational* system because it appraises job competencies from four perspectives:

1. From the perspective of an employee's manager
2. From team members (departmental employees collectively)

3. Via a self-appraisal

4. From an appraisal by the employees of their department—its environment, or culture

Each of these four appraisals is conducted using independent instruments and formal appraisal documents. In addition, a fifth system component is a document describing the feedback and reward procedures, which uses the information collected through the four appraisals. Although the exercises in this chapter are the last for the *people front*, the appraisal and feedback system is no less important than the others. And, although the feedback procedure is the last component of the appraisal system, feedback communication, as will become evident, is first in importance when it comes to quality *organizational* performance.

STANDARD 11. THE ORGANIZATIONAL APPRAISAL AND FEEDBACK SYSTEM

Goals: Develop four appraisal instruments that will be used to assess organizational performance based on job information obtained from four independently conducted appraisals: (1) employee, (2) group, (3) self, and (4) department. In addition, develop the feedback and reward procedures. The feedback procedure uses the aggregate of results from the four appraisals for discussions on ways to improve on organizational performance and to recognize and reward employees.

Specific Objectives: Develop four appraisal instruments to collect a comprehensive body of information describing the overall performance of the organization in terms of specific job tasks and information security. Next, develop a feedback protocol, or procedure, to guide discussions by employees and their managers on options for improvements, if necessary, and on the reward preferences and ways to administer them.

The specific objective is the creation of a feedback mechanism using the appraisal outcome measures to identify and intercept faulty work or job problems that impede organizational performance. Unlike financial outcome measures of organizational performance that depend in great part on external factors, such as the economy, the BISP appraisal and feedback system measures factors that are largely controllable by the company: the job tasks and the means to perform them. Routinely scheduled feedback meetings using inclusive appraisal details are essential for the BISP appraisal system and are required to comply with Standard 11.

Orientation

The primary purposes of the BISP appraisal system are to generate outcomes for communication and feedback and to recognize and reward employees for performing their security-sensitive job tasks. For employees in job positions at all levels—entry, supervisory, managerial, and any other—on-the-job performance is assumed to meet or exceed management expectations, or these employees would not be retained by the company. For *new* employees, excellent performance is guaranteed because the legally compliant BISP Standards were used in selection.

Most workers want to succeed on the job. Few want to fail or be viewed by others as a failure. When job performance falls short, the problem is most often due to the job and not the person performing the job. For example, although the job tasks for a particular job may remain the same, the technology used to perform those tasks changes rapidly. In fact, technology is often outdated before it can be implemented. As technology and techniques evolve, job performance follows a learning curve for which peak performance cannot be expected without training, either formally or self-taught while on the job.

Additionally, there are many conditions under which high performance is impossible, despite the worker's best effort. For example, employees have little or no control over job outcomes when materials are lacking or machines are malfunctioning. However, these and other root causes of poor on-the-job performance can be corrected quickly through regularly conducted feedback sessions using performance appraisal outcomes. The direct impact is on an organization's fiscal performance. Ideally, therefore, this appraisal and the feedback system is administered quarterly to intercept and immediately correct faulty workplace or job factors likely to negatively impact the company's financial outcomes.

In addition to organizational performance, the BISP appraisal system serves other purposes. For progressive companies that continuously aim for improvement, the BISP appraisal results are to be used for feedback and communication meetings to discuss ways to develop employees' skills, determine the progression of career paths, and otherwise identify issues of equal importance to the employee and the company. Further, it is human nature for individuals to want to know how they may be perceived by others and to receive the recognition they deserve for hard work and jobs well done. These innate qualities are satisfied through the BISP organizational appraisal and feedback system.

The exercises that develop this system are the last tasks to complete the standards for the people front and also the last tasks to be performed by this first project team. At the end of this chapter, the team's concluding exercise will be to help elect, select, or otherwise ensure that a new project team is in place to complete the remaining Standards in Parts II and III.

INDIVIDUAL APPRAISAL

Exercise 1. Develop the Individual Appraisal Instrument

Estimated Time: Four Hours
The appraisal instrument is a formal document enumerating the job competencies required for job positions. The items in the appraisal instrument can be used to appraise all jobs within a job set as well as specific competencies required for some job positions. (These items will be replicated below in exercises 2 and 3.) Conduct exercise 1 in two steps.

1. Prepare a list of job competencies for each job *set* within the department. The team's task has already been partly completed, because these competencies are the items identified in Chapter 9 in the job analysis. For each job competency identified in the job analysis, create a statement using as its subject a specific job task. For consistency, the example in Exhibit 17.1 uses the job competency items shown in Exhibit 9.1.

EXHIBIT 17.1 *Job Competency Appraisal Instrument*

Date of Appraisal: _____

Employee Name: _____

Employee Job Position: _____

Name of Rater_____

Rate the performance of each job competency using the following rating scale where:

          1 = Fails to meet expectations

          2 = Somewhat meets expectations

          3 = Meets expectations

          4 = Exceeds expectations

          5 = Greatly exceeds expectations

1. Maintains required certification _____
2. Routinely secures databases _____
3. Conducts information process risk assessments on schedule _____
4. Maintains security standards _____
5. Exhibits honesty _____
6. Performs job tasks consistently _____
   .
   .
   .
13. Performs job tasks on time _____

Notes: This instrument has been developed based on the job competencies identified in the Security Job Analysis. The ratings of job competencies must be made by supervisors or managers who are in positions to regularly observe the on-the-job performance of the employee or who otherwise have direct evidence that the job outcomes were performed by the employee. Overall ratings range from 13 (fails to meet expectations) to 39 (meets expectations) to 65 (greatly exceeds expectations). Ratings of 26 or lower (those less than "meets expectations") must be accompanied by tangible evidence for such ratings.

All ratings are to remain confidential with this rater or with the rater's supervisor or manager who also oversees the job performance for the above employee.

For each job set, include both general and technical job competencies. For example, if honesty is a required competency for that job set, include honesty on the list of items to be appraised. Or if the job competencies required for managerial positions concern feedback of appraisal outcomes, a job analysis would likely have identified as competencies items such as feedback, timeliness, and communication. Recognition is no less important for managers who devote the time and effort to mentor employees using the appraisal and feedback system.

2. After compiling the list of job competencies, create a rating scale for each statement. Use the five-point range depicted in Exhibit 17.1.

When completed, this set of job competency statements comprises the first of four independent appraisal instruments of the BISP Organizational Appraisal and Feedback System. When formulated based on the results of the Security Job Analysis conducted according to the instructions in Chapter 9, this (first) appraisal instrument meets Equal Economic Opportunity Commission (EEOC) compliance standards and can be used to evaluate employees individually and as the basis for job- and work-related decisions. However, most jobs today require *team* efforts for successful performance, which is why today's companies also must appraise performance at the group level of analysis. The second instrument required for Standard 11, therefore, is the group appraisal document.

GROUP APPRAISAL

Exercise 2. Develop the Group Appraisal Instrument

Estimated Time: Three Hours

Employees should have the opportunity to be rated on their performance by others who are in positions to observe the job behaviors frequently. Employees whose jobs can be objectively rated by a number of people in different positions, such as managers, other employees, and customers, can benefit from a broader range of feedback, which, recall from the earlier discussion, is the primary purpose of the appraisal and feedback system. At the very least, employees should be provided the benefits of appraisals from members of their work group and other employees in the course of performing job tasks. This group appraisal instrument serves those purposes.

Use the identical list of job competencies (created for individuals in exercise 1). Only the instructions at the top of the appraisal instrument differ: In this exercise, the directions are for group (versus individual) level of analysis, and the appraisals are to be conducted anonymously. With these exceptions, follow the same three steps as in exercise 1 to create this second instrument of the appraisal and feedback system:

1. Use the list of job competencies for each job *set* within the department.
2. Also use the rating scale for each statement using the same five-point range (depicted in Exhibit 17.2) to measure performance expectations.
3. Include a comment section at the bottom of the instrument. See Exhibit 17.2 for an example of the instructions for the work group appraisals instrument.

An inclusive appraisal and feedback system provides perspectives from multiple observation points. Therefore, in addition to appraisals conducted at the individual and group levels of analysis, a third instrument provides opportunities for self-appraisals.

SELF-APPRAISAL

Exercise 3. Develop the Self-Appraisal Instrument

Estimated Time: Two Hours
Employees should be provided the opportunity to appraise their own job competencies. Employees are closest to the job and can best determine deficiencies in procedures, practices, equipment, materials, or other factors impacting their own on-the-job performance. Indeed, often only the person holding a specific job position has insight into problems

EXHIBIT 17.2   *Work Group Appraisal Instrument*

Date of Appraisal: _____

Work Group (Team or Department Name): _____

Names of group members (include your own name):

Member 1.   _____

Member 2.   _____

Member 3.   _____

.

.

Member *n*   _____

- -

Rate the performance of each member of the work group (team) on each job competency using this rating scale where:

$$1 = \text{Fails to meet expectations}$$
$$2 = \text{Somewhat meets expectations}$$
$$3 = \text{Meets expectations}$$
$$4 = \text{Exceeds expectations}$$
$$5 = \text{Greatly exceeds expectations}$$

Also rate yourself. Do not sign your name, Social Security number, or any other personal identifying number, and do not discuss your ratings with other team members.

		Group Member Number			
		#1	#2	#3 ...	#n
1.	Maintains required certification	___	___	___	___
2.	Routinely secures databases	___	___	___	___
3.	Conducts information risk assessments on schedule	___	___	___	___
4.	Maintains security standards	___	___	___	___
5.	Exhibits honesty	___	___	___	___
6.	Performs job tasks consistently	___	___	___	___
.					
.					
.					
13.	Performs job tasks on time	___	___	___	___

- -

General Comments:

_____

_____

_____

Notes: This instrument was developed based on the job competencies identified in the Security Job Analysis. The ratings are to be conducted anonymously by each memeber of the work group (or department). Overall ratings range from 13 (fails to meet expectations) to 39 (meets expectations) to 65 (greatly exceeds expectations). Ratings of 26 or lower (those less than "meets expectations") must be accompanied by tangible evidence for such ratings.

or options for performance improvements. Such firsthand information on how to improve services and productivity is valuable for organizational performance, which is why self-appraisal is essential.

Follow the procedures described in exercise 2 (developing the group appraisal instrument): (1) duplicate the job competency list, (2) create the rating scale, and (3) redefine the instructions for conducting self-appraisals. Include a section at the bottom of this instrument for comments. When completed, move on to exercise 4.

DEPARTMENTAL ASSESSMENT

Exercise 4. Develop the Departmental Appraisal Instrument

Estimated Time: Three Hours

In Chapter 15 (Standard 9), the team generated items to describe the company's honest culture. These items were then used to formulate the Realistic Job Preview.

Use this list of items to create a departmental appraisal instrument. Follow the same format as previous exercises for the other appraisal instruments. That is, use the items to create statements, and include the same five-point rating scale. This instrument, which is to be designed as an anonymous appraisal, will measure employee perceptions of their department's work culture. The results from such appraisals are to be used together with the results from the preceding three appraisals (individual, group, and self) for discussion for improvements and *departmental* recognition and rewards.

Take five steps to develop the departmental appraisal instrument:

1. Retrieve (from Chapter 15) the list of items generated on company culture.
2. Using the items on this list, generate statements to solicit employee perceptions of how well the company's honest culture is being maintained.

3. Create the five-point rating scale.
4. At the top of the instrument, create the instructions. Be certain to include the word "anonymous."
5. At the bottom of the instrument, include a section for anonymous comments.

Upon completion of this exercise, four instruments have been developed, each designed to independently measure on-the-job performance from a unique perspective. The aggregate of information collected using these instruments will be used later to maintain organizational performance and security. To achieve these desired organizational outcomes, appraisals are to be conducted regularly on schedule with timely feedback. After the four appraisal instruments have been developed, go on to exercise 5 to establish the time plan for administering these appraisals and for conducting the feedback meetings.

Exercise 5. Develop Time Plans and Procedures

Estimated Time: Four Hours

Appraisals without feedback are like taking half a bath, playing nine holes of golf, mowing half a lawn, or working with no reward. The current need, therefore, is to develop time plans to administer the four instruments and to conduct the feedback meetings so as to (a) make procedural, mechanical, or other changes to improve organizational performance and (b) reward performance the company wishes to reinforce. To be effective, the administration of appraisal instruments and the feedback meetings must be conducted sequentially and in close temporal proximity. It is best to conceptualize this appraisal-feedback process as one seamless, overall procedure.

The time plans and procedures for administering the appraisals and conducting the feedback meetings will be unique for each company. For some companies, quarterly reviews may be too time-consuming and cost prohibitive; such reviews may be possible and practicable for smaller companies with fewer employees. Time plans also may depend on the number of departments and the number of job sets within departments, not to mention other company-specific factors. At a minimum, however, the appraisal and feedback meetings must be conducted semiannually, at firmly scheduled times each year. The continued challenge for the project team is to develop a time plan and procedure to accomplish these initiatives in the shortest time and at the least cost.

Step 1. Use the following guidelines for administering the appraisal instruments:

- Develop a specific time plan to administer the four appraisal instruments; consult with management, consider the company's calendar of other events, and select a time when most employees are likely to be available (e.g., avoiding holiday seasons and peak vacation periods).
- Develop a procedure to administer these appraisals: Use formal brainstorming to generate ideas for the most efficient and cost-effective method for administering the four appraisals. (Consider administering the appraisals using the business intranet computer system or at scheduled meetings or conferences.)
- Determine the job position or positions within a job set responsible for scoring the appraisals.
- Establish a closing date for completing the appraisal procedure.

Step 2. For the feedback meetings, follow these guidelines:

- Consider the composition of employees who will attend the meetings. As a formal rule: include in the meetings all individuals whose job performance will be discussed either individually or as members of a work (departmental) group.
- Create two distinct opportunities for feedback and communication: (1) meetings between employee and manager and (2) meetings among employees and managers who work together as a group or whose job tasks require frequent interaction.
- Specify times for these meetings, to be held as soon as possible after the appraisals have been conducted.

In terms of recognition and rewards, behavioral science research has shown that immediate reinforcement through prompt recognition increases the probability of desired behaviors. Both employees and their companies benefit from rewards that are tied into the appraisal and feedback system. Perhaps the most important people practice is the last: rewarding and recognizing valued employees.

Exercise 6. Recognize and Reward Employees

Estimated Time: Four Hours
To recognize employees, first identify their reward preferences. Generate a large list of reward preferences, based on what employees say they prefer. Consider both intrinsic and extrinsic rewards.

Intrinsic rewards come from an internal satisfaction of a job well done. Employees are assured of a job well done when managers recognize, compliment, and in other ways show appreciation. In these small but meaningful ways, managers mete out intrinsic rewards.

Extrinsic rewards are also under management's control, in the forms of salaries or wages, bonuses, benefit plans, flextime, and other work accommodations. However, employees also appreciate smaller rewards, such as certificates of recognition, an unexpected hour's early leave time, opportunities for development, or even autonomy in performing their jobs. Use this six-step procedure to develop the list of reward preferences:

1. Use formal brainstorming to generate a large list of creative ideas for rewards.
2. Organize this list of ideas using the cause-and-effect analysis and the four M's (manpower, method, machine, and materials) to generate even more creative ideas.
3. Use the list of preferences as items in a survey to determine the most preferred intrinsic and extrinsic rewards.
4. Create a 1 to 5 rating scale for each item (preferred reward), where 1 = less important and 5 = most important.

5. Provide all company employees with an opportunity to complete the survey either online or through company mail. (You might be surprised to find what many employees consider the most preferred rewards.)

6. Conduct *one last* brainstorming session. Based on the results from the survey, generate, present to management, and establish times to administer preferred rewards. (For example, many companies hold annual meetings, conferences, or other events or occasions where employees can be recognized and rewarded.)

A MESSAGE TO THE PROJECT TEAM

Congratulations! Your team has just completed a long series of rigorous and intensively intellectual and time-consuming exercises to secure the identifying information held by your company. Because of your time, energy, and efforts, the employees and customers in your company can be confident that their personal identities are safe and secure on the *people front*. I cordially invite you to attend the annual award ceremony for companies that have implemented the Business Information Security Program (BISP). The Michigan State University Partnership team will be honored to formally recognize your team's impressive accomplishments.

In conclusion, thus far in Part II, 11 BISP security standards have been developed and implemented to secure your company's people. Their security is the first line of defense for information security. You can be confident that your company's borders now are protected by employees who themselves maintain and enforce a company culture that is designed to promote security and prevent identity theft, and rightly recognizes employee performance. With business borders now secured on the people front, attention turns to the *process front*.

CHAPTER 18

THE PROCESS FRONT: SECURE BUSINESS INFORMATION PROCESSES

According to the Four-Factor Model of Information Security, all threats to information security and all information security solutions involve four valuable business assets: (1) people, (2) processes, (3) proprietary information, and (4) property (both virtual and actual). Proprietary information is any information a business holds in confidence, including marketing strategies, development plans, competitive business techniques, and the personal identifying information of its own employees and of customers. Financial and all other institutions can secure these forms of proprietary business information by securing their people, processes, and property.

In the preceding chapters, the first project team developed Security Standards that, when implemented and maintained, are guaranteed to secure the *people front* from thefts of proprietary information, including the personal identities of customers and employees.

The goals for the second project team (composed of employees from the same department), described here through Chapter 22, are to:

1. Secure the process front.

2. Secure the property front—the virtual Web site.
3. Create a customer assistance program for victims of identity theft.
4. Develop an extensive list of e-commerce "best practices" for customers.
5. Design identity theft legislation that promotes a competitive advantage and does not impact a company's budget or business operations.

Additionally, Chapter 23, dedicated to healthcare and healthcare-related institutions, provides an overview of the standards and procedures used to secure the national identity database created by the Health Insurance Portability and Accountability Act (HIPAA). This is a tall order! However, the team approach works quite well, and step-by-step instructions will guide you.

Before continuing, however, it's time to select a new project team. *This team must be comprised of employees and managers from the same department as the first project team,* because the exercises in the remaining chapters continue from preceding chapters—and continuity within the department is imperative for security.

SELECT A NEW PROJECT TEAM

Goal: Elect, select, or seek volunteers for a new project team who will develop Standards 12–16 (and Standard 17 for healthcare-related institutions) to secure business information processes and the company's virtual property.

Specific Objectives: Identify a minimum of three and a maximum of five employees and one or more managers from the same (or cross-functional or otherwise interrelated) departments as for the first project team. The team members must be employees whose job positions enable them to commit to regularly scheduled weekly meetings for three to four hours each week for the duration of the project. To select the new project team, follow the specific instructions in steps 1 and 2 in the orientation.

Orientation

First, carefully review and then complete the instructions in each of the following steps to determine the composition of the new project team and to learn how to use the quality-to-security management tools for developing the final series of Security Standards for the Business Information Security Program (BISP).

Step 1. Read Chapter 6 in its entirety: the "Message to Executives" and the "Message to Employees." These pages describe the four conditions required to successfully develop the Security Standards.

Step 2. Create the project team. Create a team of volunteered, selected, or elected employees who, with input from other company employees, will develop the Security Standards. The team is to be composed of a minimum of three and a maximum of five employees, including at least one manager. Team members are to be from the same department as the first project team, as the exercises in the remaining chapters follow from and use the results of all preceding exercises.

Each team member is to hold a different job position because the BISP exercises require a breadth of knowledge about the jobs and job tasks within a department. However, it is not necessary to represent all job positions within a department. Team members should be longer-tenured employees who, relative to more recent hires, should have superior knowledge of the business, its jobs, and work processes. When assembling this team and for continuity, identify employees whose job positions are most likely to enable them to meet consistently at the same time and the same day each week throughout the several weeks of the project.

The new project team will complete the exercises for the remaining chapters. As discussed in an earlier chapter, comprehensive security requires the securing of people, processes, proprietary information, and property *for all company departments*. However, the BISP can be rolled out consecutively by department, or the program can be developed concurrently by multiple departments, each with its own two project teams. Small businesses with few employees may require only one team to secure the four fronts for the entire business.

If departments are implementing the BISP concurrently, each department is to, at this time, elect, select, or seek volunteers for the second project team. In so doing, first follow the prerequisites for team composition listed in Appendix B. Take time now to review Appendix B. Then create the new project team. Before beginning, learn about the quality-to-security tools that are used to create the Security Standards.

QUALITY-TO-SECURITY TOOLS

Step 3. The first series of Standards (1-11) were developed using formal brainstorming and cause-and-effect analysis, two quality management tools adapted by the BISP for security. Each of these tools will be used again to develop the remaining Security Standards. In addition, these remaining Standards require two additional quality-to-security tools: flow charting and Pareto analysis. The results obtained from formal brainstorming are used to conduct the cause-and-effect analysis, and the results of the cause-and-effect analysis are then used for flow charting and to perform the Pareto analysis. Each of these quality-to-security management tools is described later in this chapter, and all were designed for *team* problem solving. Additionally, each tool has its own specific conditions and step-by-step instructions.

Any deviations from these requirements, such as devising shortcuts, will jeopardize the accomplishments gained in preceding chapters and the Business Information Security Program itself. Before continuing, therefore, each team member is to carefully review the procedures for applying the problem-solving tools that follow.

Step 4. Brainstorm! Brainstorming is a method used to generate an extensive list of ideas that can be used to solve problems. *Formal* brainstorming is specific in its approach. Carefully read the instructions for formal brainstorming in Appendix C. Review also Exhibit C.1, which shows a sample brainstorming problem statement created by a team working on a bioterrorism contingency plan. For the sake of illustration, Exhibit C.2 lists the results of a formal brainstorming session conducted by a team at the headquarters of a major automaker in Detroit. For the BISP, the brainstorming is highly structured and formal. It is important to guard against relaxing this procedure; deviations will undermine the quality of the results needed for security.

Step 5. Conduct a cause-and-effect analysis. Cause-and-effect analysis is used to organize and build on ideas generated through formal brainstorming. Appendix D describes in detail the step-by-step instructions for conducting cause-and-effect analysis and emphasizes the importance in the analysis of using the four M's: manpower, methods, machines, and materials. Appendix D describes the cause-and-effect method and Exhibits D.1 and D.2 graphically illustrate it. Appendix D and related exhibits are taken from an actual case. In the exhibits, the project team was in the process of identifying the entry points of identities into the department and also the possible sources of identity thefts once identities were inside their department. Take time to now carefully read the instructions in Appendix D and examine the fishbone diagrams in Exhibit D.1 and D.2 for organizing and building on the ideas generated in the formal brainstorming.

Step 6. Perform flow chart analysis. Flow charting is the quality-to-security tool used to trace the input-throughput-output of information (e.g., identities) through a department by tracing the sequence of job tasks performed in a work process that utilizes that information. Most or all work processes follow both a paper trail and a digital trail. An example is when a patron deposits money with a teller at a drive-in bank, which triggers a series of job tasks.

Initial procedures—the job tasks of the bank clerk—require and use the personal identifiers, such as name, address, Social Security and bank account number, to identify, verify, and retrieve the customer's file from the bank database. The record of deposit is then entered into the database. A paper receipt is printed for the customer. Then the transaction is recorded on a bank statement, which is mailed to the patron, usually at the end of the month.

The steps throughout this financial transaction represent an *informa-tion process*. These steps involving a single bank deposit can involve at least five (or more) job tasks that are performed in at least two (or more) different job positions—and each of these five or more job tasks can be ordered sequentially from beginning (the deposit) to end (the bank state-ment). *Flow-charting lays out visually this information process.*

Flow-charting always follows the process through job positions and *not the people who hold those positions.* Job positions are relatively sta-ble whereas people come and go. Moreover, it is the *process* that is to be secured.

Appendix I defines, describes, and illustrates information processes and how to illustrate them. Exhibit I.1 shows 12 of the most commonly used standardized engineering symbols—the universal language for in-terpreting flow charts. Exhibit I.2 shows how one team in the Leasing Department's Vehicle Inventory Unit of a major U.S. automaker traced orders that are routinely faxed into that unit. These documents contain identifying information including the name, Social Security number, and driver's license number of the individual requesting the lease (or sometimes purchase) of an automobile. At this time, carefully review Appendix I and Exhibits I.1 and I.2.

Step 7. Perform the Pareto analysis. The results from brainstorming are used to conduct cause-and-effect analysis; the results from cause-and-effect analysis are used for flow-charting; and the results of flow-charting are used for Pareto analysis. Just as the chapters in this book build on one another, so, too, do these four quality-to-security tools. This step intro-duces the last tool, the Pareto analysis.

Pareto analysis is a two-step procedure. First, the analysis prioritizes problems identified in the cause-and-effect analysis and the flow chart, in order of importance. The location in an information process where threat of identity theft is the greatest is also the most important problem and the first in order of priority to be secured. Second, the Pareto *dia-gram*, a simple bar chart that lists the frequencies of potential threats to a location, is created. The Pareto analysis *quality* control tool, adapted by the BISP for *security* control, is defined, described, and illustrated in Appendix J. Take time now to review Appendix J. Then continue on with the exercises below to complete Standard 12, the Information Process Risk Assessment.

STANDARD 12. INFORMATION PROCESS RISK ASSESSMENT

Standard 12 calls for a risk assessment to be conducted on information processes within a department. The new project team is to use the results obtained from the analysis conducted in Chapter 8 by the first project team. In that chapter, the first project team developed lists of "personal" and "business" identities and the sources of those identities into the department. It is these sources that are the subjects in the first exercise here, using the previously described quality-to-security tools.

Goal: Conduct an information process risk assessment on information processes within the department to secure the process from threats of identity theft.

Specific Objectives: There are four objectives.

1. Identify incoming sources of identities into the department—personal (employee and customer) or business, or both. Do one category of identity at a time (e.g., personal then business). For ease in discussion and descriptions, it is hereafter assumed that the focus of attention is on *personal* identities.
2. Trace the flow of the identifying information as it is processed through the department by tracing the documents that contain such information.
3. Determine the locations in the process where the identities are most susceptible to theft.
4. Secure this information process—the input–throughput–output process—in which job tasks on a document (e.g., loan application) are sequentially performed by different job positions within a department.

Orientation

To complete Standard 12, the Information Process Risk Assessment, first follow steps 3 through 7 in the orientation given above. Then go on to exercise 1.

Exercise 1. Identify Sources of Personal Identities

Estimated Time: This exercise was completed by the first project team. Obtain from team 1 the list of incoming sources of personal identities. If this exercise 2 (in Chapter 8) had not already been completed, use these instructions:

> Use structured brainstorming to determine where the identities first come into the department. To do so, generate a list of all present and future potential sources of incoming sources of information. Focus on the places or *locations* where information first enters the department. For example, if information is sent through the mail and the mail is delivered to a location in the department, that location—desk, mailbox, or other—is the first *source* and the entry point into the information process. Information (e.g., identities) can also come into the department by fax, phone, e-mail, or other internal or external memos, letters, or other sources.

The information process risk assessment concerns information *within a department.* What occurs with the information *before* it arrives or *after* it leaves the department is not in the process and is, therefore, not in the control of the department. To the extent that the information is processed *across* departments, the security of the information depends on information process risk assessment being conducted in those departments as well. Use the lists of incoming sources of personal identities in exercise 2.

Exercise 2. Track the Flow

Estimated Time: Three Hours
For each source—the entry point of information into the department, the "input" stage in the process—on the list (exercise 1), use flow-charting to

trace the identity as it is processed through the department. That is, trace the input-throughput-output flow of a document, statement, or other form that carries personal identities.

An important note: Be certain to distinguish between *how* the information is processed and *where* it is processed. For example, *how* refers to verb terms such as "distribute," "deliver," and "sort," and *where* refers to nouns such as "desk," "mailbox," and "computer." Thus, an identity theft could occur during distribution, delivery, or sorting, or by taking from a desk, mailbox, or computer. The author suggests using the nouns—the where, the sequential job positions where identifying information is worked on; that is, where tasks are performed using the identities. See Appendix I, Exhibit I.2, for a simplified example of locations in a flow chart. These job positions or locations are the first to be secured and then the transfer paths between the locations can be secured.

To continue, follow the document (containing the identity) beginning at its source and through the job positions that perform the standard job tasks on this type of document (e.g., loan applications). Generate an input-throughput-output flow chart using the standardized engineering symbols, the universal language for interpreting flow charts, presented in Appendix I, Exhibit I.1.

Exercise 3. Locate Weaknesses in the Information Process

Estimated Time: Three Hours

This exercise uses the quality-to-security tools interchangeably. That is, building on the flow chart analysis from the last exercise, proceed to apply formal brainstorming at each point in the flow chart process to generate as many ideas as possible as to how personal information could be subjected to theft at that location in the process. Use the flip chart, create the task statement, and follow the rules for personal time and the round robin. Perform this exercise now.

Next, building on the results of the brainstorming, conduct a cause-and-effect analysis to organize the brainstorming ideas along the four M's: manpower, methods, machine, and materials. Review, if necessary the cause-and-effect procedure in the above orientation. Refer also to

Exhibits D.1 and D.2 in Appendix D for the cause-and-effect analysis that was conducted by one company's team. Note in the exhibits that the *cause* is one of the four M's and the *effect* is the identity theft. Remember, the task now is to organize the target points or locations according to the cause.

To illustrate by way of a further example, if a driver's license number is sent into the department for verification using e-mail, the possible threats to the theft of this identity may be one or all of the following: manpower (allowing others to use the computer); an unsecured machine (spyware on the computer); materials (unsecured hard copy of the e-mail message); or method—unencrypted or intercepted e-mail. Each of these four—manpower, machine, materials, and method—is the potential root source of the theft of the identity: name, address, Social Security number, bank account, credit card, or other. Systematically recognizing and analyzing the four M's after initial brainstorming based on a flow chart analysis almost always reveals additional weaknesses in the information process. When completed, go on to the next exercise, the Pareto analysis.

Exercise 4. Prioritize Weaknesses in the Process

Estimated Time: Four Hours

Pareto analysis is used to analyze the results obtained from flow-charting and the cause-and-effect analysis. Use the columnar format depicted in Appendix J. List each incoming source in column 1. Create headings for the locations to be secured. In Appendix J, the location is described in terms of the sequential job positions through which the identity was "worked on," or processed. Include a heading for Frequencies: the number of places in the process that the document passes through. In Appendix J, for example, the U.S. mail document passed through three locations. Next, simply for ease in visualizing the most important locations to be secured, transfer this information to a bar chart, using again the example in Appendix J. The bar chart is the basis for exercise 5—securing the information process.

Exercise 5. Secure the Information Process

Estimated Time: Four Hours

So far, the route through the department of a document containing identifying information has been determined, as have the vulnerable weak points in this process. It is now time to secure the process. Use formal brainstorming to generate a comprehensive list of creative ideas as to how each location in the process might be secured. Be certain to use the flip chart, create the task statement, and follow the rules for personal time and for conducting the round robin (as described in Appendix C). Then organize this list of ideas using cause-and-effect analysis. The goal in the cause-and-effect analysis is to identify mechanisms or methods by which each of the items listed under the four M's can be secured.

Exercise 6. Develop a Time Plan

Estimated Time: Three Hours

The results of the information process risk assessment are useless without a time plan to implement them. Upon completing exercise 5, agree by team discussion and consensus on short- and long-term time plans to implement the security mechanisms. Appendix H presents one company's strategic plan for implementing mechanisms for security. Many short-term plans can be put into effect immediately without much time, effort, or other costs. Longer-term plans may require budgeting and formal approval from upper management. Be realistic and specific with target dates. Present the final results to management as recommendations for action.

In conclusion, the *process* front now has been secured; that is, security mechanisms are in place for the work processes used to manage and maintain personal identifying information. It is now time to turn attention to the *property* front—that is, the *virtual* property, the company's Web site. E-shopping is not the wave of the future—it is here now. To maintain a competitive advantage and remain financially stable, today's businesses must provide consumers with opportunities for e-shopping and online experiences that are perceived as safe and secure.

Unfortunately, consumers are increasingly reluctant to shop online for fear of identity theft. Much depends, however, on a customer's *perception* of security while shopping online. In the next chapter, the team's task is to ensure that customers feel safe when conducting business on your company's Web site.

With the completion of this chapter's exercises, the second project team has completed its first Security Standard—the process front. The next task is to secure the property front—the company's e-commerce Web site.

CHAPTER 19

THE PROPERTY FRONT: THE E-BUSINESS WEB SITE

How safe do e-shoppers feel when they visit your Web site? All businesses conduct employee performance evaluations either formally as part of an annual review or informally during day-to-day operations. However, few companies, if any, assess the performance of their Web sites with respect to customer perceptions of security. For e-businesses, a customer's assessment of the security of a Web site could provide critical information, which is the purpose of Standard 13.

STANDARD 13. WEB SITE SECURITY ASSESSMENT

Customers are the users of the e-business Web sites. Potential customers might use the sites if they perceive that their information is secured. The customer, therefore, whether an online shopper or not, is in the best position to inform the company of perceptions of security. In addition, by offering customers an opportunity to help secure their own privacy, your company conveys the message that it cares.

Goals: Develop a Web site security assessment, then administer the assessment to internal employees and to volunteer customers.

Specific Objectives: This standard aims to measure the performance of the company Web site in terms of customer perceptions of security for conducting e-business and to solicit new ideas from those customers for improvements that might create a broader sense of security for e-shopping.

Exercise 1. Develop the Web Site Security Assessment

Estimated Time: Three Hours

Solicit and invite participation of a group of 5 to 10 company employees (other than the project team) from a cross section of departments for formal brainstorming and a focus group interview. The task is to use structured brainstorming followed by a group interview to generate the largest possible list of ideas that will make e-shoppers feel secure when using the company Web site.

Depending on their use of Web sites for conducting e-business and their knowledge of computer and network security, employees from a wide range of departments will generate different ideas. People with little or no knowledge of computers or e-shopping practices often offer new and unique ideas because they are not thinking "within the box." The list of ideas can include technical methods for securing the Web site, but the ultimate goal is to generate new and creative visual or verbal messages that portray your company's sincerity for customer security. This exercise is conducted in three steps.

Step 1. Conduct formal brainstorming with three groups of company employees: two groups of volunteer employees from various departments and the third, the project team. Before beginning, elect a project member to carefully review with the two new groups the step-by-step instructions for formal brainstorming (Appendix C). Carefully follow these instructions using a flip chart for each team, the task statement, personal think time without discussion, the numerical listing of ideas on the flip chart, and the round robin. (Remember, the round robin is the disciplined procedure in which each person reports an idea generated during the personal think time; the recorder lists the idea on the flip chart; the next person reports an idea; and so forth, without discussion, until all ideas, including new ones triggered in the round robin, are exhausted.) Emphasize during the instructions an anything-goes approach, and encourage piggyback-ing on others' ideas to trigger new ideas. Challenge the teams to generate the largest possible list of creative ideas for Web site security.

Step 2. When the brainstorming exercise is finished, invite each team in turn to present their findings to the other two groups. After all presenta-tions are made, use a fourth flip chart sheet to consolidate items generated by the three teams, eliminating duplicated items.

Step 3. Now use the items on this fourth sheet as the basis for a focus group interview using the four-M framework to guide the group discus-sion. The object is to prompt group members to think about *how* each idea on the list might be implemented; that is, to discuss options for prac-tical applications. Before beginning, carefully review the rationale for using the four-M framework.

A typical agenda for this exercise might be:

8:00–8:30	Coffee and introductions
8:30–9:00	Instructions for structured and formal brainstorming
9:00–10:00	Conduct formal brainstorming
10:00–10:15	Break
10:15–11:15	Team presentations
11:15–12:00	Focus interview and discussion based on the four M's

Feedback is important. Describe to the volunteer teams how their ideas are to be used to develop the Web site document, and after the assessment has been administered (exercise 2), make certain to inform each of these employees of the final results.

Exercise 2. Web Site Security Assessment

Estimated Time: Two Hours
Use the team approach and, in the next four steps, create and adminis-ter the Web site assessment and interpret the results.

Step 1. Use the ideas from exercise 1 and the example in Exhibit 19.1 to create a Web site security assessment. Administer the Web site assessment first to internal customers (employees) not involved in its development for their additions or other modifications. Administer the assessment to employees in the form that it will be administered to customers. For example, if the project team decides to administer the final document online, then administer the assessment to employees online as well. Allow one to two weeks for employee responses. Then through team discussion and consensus, evaluate and integrate into the assessment document pertinent items or details that make further contributions.

Step 2. Next, administer the final Web site security assessment online, in paper-and-pencil format through U.S. mail, to customers who visit the on-site store, or use a combination of these or other options. Select from the company database and invite participation from a large group of volunteers who are *current customers*, including customers who do not yet use the company Web site for their business transactions.

Or administer the assessment through U.S. mail to a random sample of customers, or as part of a marketing campaign to inform and attract e-customers. Consider offering a coupon or some other form of compensation for customer participation. Note that this Web site security assessment is intended for use as an in-house document in which the *customer*, as distinguished from the *consumer*, is considered an insider.

Step 3. Score the results. To determine the Web site features that give customers the most and least sense of security, sum each item (the Web site feature) across all returned assessments and then order the items in terms of priority from high to low.

For example, if 100 customers participated and all selected "5" for the item "Seal of Information Security," the highest possible score for that item would be 500. Alternatively, the lowest score for any given item would be 100, and the midrange score would be 300. Use this continuum as a benchmark to interpret the results, to order the items according to their relative scores, and to then identify items that could be

EXHIBIT 19.1   *Example of a Web Site Security Assessment*

The Web Site Assessment

We wish to create for our customers the most functional and secure Web site on the Internet. To do this, we seek your help. Our customers are in the best positions to give us their perceptions of privacy and security for conducting business online. For the list below, please select the number on the scale that best indicates the most or least sense of security you feel for each item.

Before beginning, review the list of items to determine which are more or less important to you. Then when completing the assessment, do not deliberate for any length of time on the rating for an item. Select the number on the scale that first comes to mind.

The Sense of Security Scale

1 = Low
2 = Moderately Low
3 = Indifferent
4 = Moderately High
5 = High

The Web Site Feature	Feature Provides a Sense of Security
	Select One
1. Testimonials from e-business customers	1 2 3 4 5
2. Pictures of company officers	1 2 3 4 5
3. Name and address of CEO	1 2 3 4 5
4. Security letter from CEO	1 2 3 4 5
5. Security letter from company employees	1 2 3 4 5
6. Seal of Information Security (the Standards)	1 2 3 4 5
7. Statement of Security Standard Compliance	1 2 3 4 5
8. Press release announcing the Security Standards	1 2 3 4 5
9. Better Business Bureau Online Reliability Seal	1 2 3 4 5
10. TRUSTe Seal	1 2 3 4 5
11. Privacy Policy	1 2 3 4 5
12. Return Policy	1 2 3 4 5
13. Picture of a lock at bottom of screen	1 2 3 4 5
. . .	1 2 3 4 5

We appreciate any comments you may offer in the space provided below.

Thank You!

included, emphasized, or omitted on the company Web site, based on customers' perceptions of security.

When interpreting the results, watch for outliers—extreme scores that are either low or high. Outliers can be especially informative and therefore should be considered carefully. Consider also the open-ended responses customers may have provided at the end of the assessment. Customers who are willing to take the time may be offering particularly important suggestions.

Step 4. Follow up. Think about a performance appraisal of you or of someone you know after which no recognition was given or no changes were made in pay, promotion, or job situation, despite work well done. Apply the knowledge from these experiences to the Web site assessment. Whenever possible, make the improvements suggested by the customer assessments or comments. Be sure to conclude by sending an online coupon or some other form of compensation or recognition along with a personalized "thank you."

Not only does this Web site security assessment provide your company with valuable information for encouraging new and continued e-business shopping practices by current customers, it also is a marketing tool that, when implemented, is sure to attract *new* customers. After all, your project team and your company's employees created the innovative Web site features that produced the results, and the power and effectiveness of group synergy cannot be underestimated.

To summarize thus far: Between the two project teams, the personal identifying information of employees and customers has been secured on three fronts—people, processes, and property. In effect, the security of people, processes, and property—including information technology security (covered widely in other texts)—comprehensively secures the fourth front: the proprietary information. Now it is time to go beyond the competition.

PART III

MONITORING IDENTITY THEFT

Go beyond the competition.

—Judith's Maxim

CHAPTER 20

THE CUSTOMER
SECURITY
PROGRAM

At the time this book was first drafted, no financial or other institution was known to offer customer assistance programs for customers who became victims of identity theft. Since then, and only in recent months, the nation's largest banking institution, CitiCorp, launched its identity theft customer call center. As of this writing, Citi is blanketing the market with thoughtful and eye-catching identity theft advertisements.

The author spent some time at CitiCorp's New York headquarters consulting on its identity theft program. I evaluated Citi's customer call center protocol, reviewed the impressive Citi Tool Kit of helpful information for victims, and taped interviews for satellite announcements of Citi's identity theft program. All businesses, regardless of size, type, or location, could follow Citi's progressive lead, because identity theft is here to stay. But to be successful, not all programs must be as elaborate as Citi's.

This chapter lays out a simple, inexpensive, and easy-to-implement eight-step customer security program that has a proven track record of success. The program is based on practices developed in the Identity Theft Lab at Michigan State University (MSU). The program evolved, since 1999, from experiences working with hundreds of identity theft victims and their families. These victims include company employees, corporate officers, college students, parents of younger children whose identities were stolen, young couples, retirees, elderly people, and people of many different races and ages, touching all walks of life, from across the United States and Europe.

The customer security program proposed here for your company is based on information compiled from these many interactions with victims, conducted by faculty and staff over countless hours in one-on-one sessions at the MSU Laboratory, over the telephone, and via U.S. and e-mail. From these many victims, we learned about the process of healing, which is applied as the basis for the customer security program.

The theory and practice of the process of healing is not new with this chapter. It was first published in *Identity Theft First Responder Manual for Criminal Justice Professionals: Police Officers, Attorneys, and Judges* [1] and is now used in police departments across the country to help officers understand and work with identity theft victims.

You can readily and easily adapt a customer security program for your company from methods that now are used successfully by hundreds of police officers and other criminal justice professionals. Reinvention is unnecessary. The eight steps in the customer security program proposed here adapt materials from the *First Responder* text, which is recommended as your resource for Standard 14.

STANDARD 14. CUSTOMER SECURITY PROGRAM

Goal: To adapt the methods described in the *Identity Theft First Responder Manual* to a customer security program for your company.

Specific Objectives: To provide employees, customers, and their families who have become victims of identity theft with: (1) needed resources for the first four crucial steps to recover financially, (2) instructions for collecting information that will help the investigation, and (3) practical steps toward the process of healing.

Orientation

The customer security program consists of eight steps of instructions that a company victim advocate would follow in instructing victims on a series of exercises to perform to help in the recovery from identity theft. These eight steps also can be used for seminar presentations, company workshops, community awareness programs presented for public service by your company, or an online customer security program. Before using this program, it is helpful to be aware of the reactions of victims upon learning of the theft of their identities.

Research on Victims of Identity Theft

The MSU Identity Theft Partnerships for Prevention recently conducted focus group interviews with male and female executives whose identifying data were stolen from a company's payroll records. Using the executives' identities, the perpetrators created bogus checks and credit cards, which they used to purchase a wide variety of goods and services from companies across the United States.

In addition to these executive data, the partnership faculty also collected data on the emotional health of male and female identity theft victims ranging in age from 23 to 76 years. The identity theft victims consistently reported a number of common emotions.

The majority of victims were fearful when they first learned of the identity theft. Fearing the unknown, these victims did not yet know the extent of the crime or whether the perpetrator had also victimized a spouse, children, parents, or other family members. Females frequently, and males less often, expressed an offensive and repugnant feeling of being personally violated by some unknown person, somewhere.[2]

These expressions of personal intrusion often were followed with feelings of despair and helplessness: There was little the victim could do, and law enforcement would not help. (In recent years, law enforcement, though lacking resources, has begun to take identity theft complaints.) As a result of the feeling of helplessness and the related sense of having no control over the situation, victims commonly become frustrated—an emotion often exacerbated by difficulties victims encounter when trying to resolve credit issues with insensitive company representatives. Anger can develop from unrelieved frustration, and anger is a precursor to depression. In the MSU Identity Theft Lab, we have seen victims at all stages of emotions, including individuals suffering from clinical depression.

Additionally, most victims reported a lack of trust—for coworkers, friends, and acquaintances and for companies where they had used their personal information. They also reported distrust of using personal information for future purchases of goods and services.

We learned from our work that although victims commonly suffer similar emotions, they do not suffer them to the same extent. While the common emotions are the same for most, recovery depends on the type of crime that was committed using the stolen identity, the extent of financial loss to the victim, and individual differences in psychological "hardiness" whereby some victims recover more quickly than others.

We later discovered an interesting phenomenon. Victims who began working on the exercises given them in the ID Theft Lab (subsequently reported in the *First Responder Manual*) circumvented the experienced emotions, usually at the point of helplessness. Although many of these individuals became frustrated and angry at the situation, and sometimes at insensitive company representatives, we have since seen no extreme cases of psychological distress for victims we have assisted. Although this revelation occurred over time, it was not surprising. Considerable research in social psychology indictates that people need a sense of control over their destinies and even the moment, in anticipation of how to act or react to a person or an event. When we aided victims to gain control through exercises to help resolve their identity theft issues and uncover relevant information for law enforcement investigations, these individuals no longer felt helpless. To help them avoid frustration, we now even alert victims to what they might expect when trying to resolve a credit issue with some company's uncaring employee. By eliminating antecedent emotions, the others on the continuum, ranging from the initial fear to helplessness, anger, and depression, can be mitigated if not prevented.

Ultimately, most, if not all, victims of identity theft reach the acceptance stage. That is, they come to accept that, although someone still may have their identifying information and someday they may be victimized again, these victims have performed the exercises for protection, and there is no longer a need for fear. Here is how the advocacy process works for each victim.

Eight-Step Customer Security Program

Estimated Time: 30 Minutes per Victim
The process of healing, and the customer security program, is comprised of a series of exercises that victims must perform on their own. Your company's victim advocate must:

1. Listen to the victim's story.
2. Express concern.
3. Provide brief instructions for the eight steps the victim must take to protect the future flow of personal information.

From experience with hundreds of victims, we know that this meeting with a victim can take from 15 to 20 minutes and can be conducted online, over the phone, by e-mail or U.S. mail, or in person on a one-to-one basis.

The series of exercises and all instructional information are based on material previously published in the *First Responder Manual* and its small paperback companion, *The Victims' Assistance Guide*, and cannot be reprinted here.[3] However, the exercises and the process of healing is so effective for victims that it can become the standard for customer security for every company willing to provide victim advocacy and to obtain the *Victim's Guide* from Amazon.com or direct from Looseleaf Law Publications (1-800-647-5547). The list price is $3.95. Purchased in bulk to provide copies for victims (or for customers to avoid becoming victimized), the *Guide* can be obtained for nominal cost.

The effort and expense is negligible relative to the potential loss of even one customer who has been victimized and who may otherwise close all business accounts, including yours. Moreover, your company also may wish to invest in a marketing plan to attract new e-shopping as well as in-store customers by proactively promoting your new Customer Security Program.

Since the material cannot be republished here, I urge the project team to obtain and use the *Guide* to create a standardized document for working with victims of identity theft.

Eight-Step Customer Security Program: A Standardized Document

Step 1. First, listen to the victim's story. Victims of identity theft often suffer equally as much as do victims of other types of crimes. By simply listening and informing the victim that help is available, the advocate conveys a message of concern.

Step 2. Spend a few minutes reviewing the first few paragraphs that provide the instructions for the "Process of Healing" (found on p. 5 in the *Guide*). Inform victims that the exercises that will help reconcile and resolve the financial, emotional, and other losses may take as many as 40 hours or more, but that each exercise is important for recovery. Recommend that victims purchase a notebook before beginning the journey, to record information they uncover through the exercises and to make notes on potential evidence for the police investigation.

Step 3. Instruct victims that, if they have not already done so, they should perform the next tasks as soon as possible and in the following order:

1. File a complaint with the police department: Identity theft is a crime.
2. Contact each of the credit bureau agencies: TransUnion, Equifax, and Experian. (Complete contact information is given in the *Guide*.)
3. Contact the bank and place a password on all banking and other financial accounts. (The *Guide* gives specific instructions on passwords.)

4. Contact credit card and all other businesses they have accounts with, placing passwords on those accounts as well.

Step 4. Discuss with victims the findings of the MSU Identity Theft Lab that show that most victims experience the same continuum of emotions to one degree or another. Emphasize also that such emotions can be short-lived for victims who become actively involved in their own financial and emotional recovery.

Step 5. The *Guide* lists dozens of other contacts victims may need to make depending on the type of identity crime. For instance, if the crime involved fraudulent or stolen checks, check verification companies should be notified. If the crime involved securities transactions, the U.S. Securities and Exchange Commission (SEC) must be informed. If the perpetrator used a driver's license with the victim's name, the state department of motor vehicles must be contacted. Victims should make these and/or many other contacts listed in the *Guide*.

Step 6. Inform victims of the importance of obtaining a credit report every six months for at least the next two years, from each of the credit reporting agencies—each report may contain different information. Describe how information on a credit report can be a tip-off for identity theft. For most identity crimes, the present address on a victim's credit report is the perpetrator's post office box or other mailing address where the fraudulently ordered credit card or merchandise is to be delivered. The *Guide* contains all information on how to read and interpret credit reports, so advocates need not review that material with victims.

Step 7. Victims should be advised to write many letters: to correct personal information on credit reports, request businesses remove fraudulent charges from accounts, dispute fraudulent charges with credit bureaus, and so forth. Each of these letters requires victims to submit specific information, and the *Guide* provides a form for each letter.

Step 8. Finally, when all stops have been put in place to prevent further victimization, victims can begin collecting information to assist the police in an investigation. Police departments, due to lack of resources, often do not investigate identity thefts. However, from considerable experience, the author knows that if the police are provided with enough pertinent information that leads to a suspect or ties the case to another, the chances are good for an investigation. This is where victims become invaluable to investigators, by recording information about the identity theft, including: when the theft was first discovered; how it was discovered; recent phone calls, e-mails, or other contacts in which victims disclosed identifying information; when victims last used a health card, driver's license, and other pertinent identification.

The *First Responder Manual* includes a section on the types of background information needed for an identity theft investigation. An important note, however: *Victims must not engage in self-help by making phone calls or other contacts with individuals suspected of the identity theft.* This is police work. The victims' role is to assist the police investigation, not to operate it. Emphasize to victims the array of ways identities are susceptible to theft. The *Guide* provides victims with an exhaustive checklist of preventive security precautions.

CONCLUSION

A customer security program need not require a phone bank or call center, or the development of an expensive portfolio of bound brochures or slick documents. All that is necessary is the implementation of a simple eight-step program to help *guide* victims to help themselves.

Your company's program can use materials in already published documents, including the *Guide* but also others. As another alternative, for each of the eight steps, the project team can conduct an Internet search on that step's topic to generate volumes of public domain literature on whom to contact, where, and what steps to take toward recovery. For example, the Federal Trade Commission (FTC)[1] is an excellent resource. In the next chapter, customers learn to use your "best practices" to prevent identity theft.

CHAPTER 21

E-COMMERCE "BEST PRACTICES" FOR CUSTOMERS

Consumers are frustrated by the lack of protection of their personal information. Most companies will not acknowledge they have been victims of identity theft for fear they will lose customers. However, within the past year especially, the flag of identity theft awareness has been raised high, and consumers now know that no business is exempt. An open letter to acknowledge the threat of identity theft and inform consumers of your company's Security Standards will impart the message that you care and have done something about it. In this chapter, the project team extends consumers an invitation to security using three practical, cost efficient, and easy to implement business approaches.

STANDARD 15. E-COMMERCE "BEST PRACTICES"

Goals: (1) Develop a list of e-shopping "best practices" for consumers, (2) compose "invitation to security" letters to consumers, (3) create a company Web page titled "E-Commerce Best Practices for Our Customers."

Specific Objectives: The objectives for Standard 15 are to develop three marketing tools, or invitations to security. First, develop an exhaustive list of e-shopping "best practices" for security. Next, create a series of one-paragraph letters announcing how your company protects its customers and employees on four business fronts: people, process, property, and (thereby) proprietary information. Finally, use the letters and the list of security best practices for a Web page titled "E-Commerce Best Practices for Our Customers."

Orientation

The three exercises for this Standard require structured and formal brainstorming followed by cause-and-effect analysis using the four M's—manpower, method, machine, and materials. For efficiency in time and effect when conducting the exercises, continue to carefully follow the instructions for using these quality-to-security tools.

Exercise 1. Develop E-Commerce Best Practices

Estimated Time: Three Hours
In step 1 and using the team approach, conduct structured and formal brainstorming to generate a list of "best practices" for consumers when e-shopping. In step 2, review your company's current Web site—in a subsequent exercise you will add the new "best practices" page. This list (created below in step 1) will be used for a series of letters in exercise 2 and for the creation of a Web page in exercise 3. The list also may be used later as a marketing tool for company newsletters, flyers, inserts for billing statements, and other business applications

Step 1. Use these points as a start for developing a list of e-shopping best practices.

- Know the merchant. Otherwise, verify and confirm the merchant's authenticity with the Better Business Bureau in that city or state.
- Even if you know the merchant, be certain the Web site is secure. Look for a graphic, such as a lock, at the bottom right corner of your browser bar.

- Before conducting business online, carefully read the company's privacy policy. Beware if there is no privacy policy. You need to know how the company will use your personal information.
- Never give bank account numbers or Social Security numbers to online merchants.
- Shop with a low-limit credit card used only for online shopping.
- What is the company's return policy? Where are returns sent? Make sure the company Web site lists complete contact information: name, phone number, address, and the name of a contact person.
- Does the company Web site provide a toll-free telephone number? Call this number to verify the authenticity of the contact information.
- Shipping and handling charges vary widely from merchant to merchant. Verify these fees before ordering merchandise.
- Be a comparison shopper. Visit several Web sites to compare prices and added fees.
- Print a copy of the purchase order showing the confirmation number, in the event of lost merchandise.
- Does the Web site display the "Seal of Information Security," indicating consumer identities are protected by the Business Information Security Program (BISP) Security Standards?
- Does the merchant's Web site display the BBB OnLine Reliability Seal? Or the TRUSTe seal? Although these seals do not guarantee security, companies that purchase them are usually legitimate.

Now increment this list with additional ideas: visit the Federal Trade Commission's Web site at *www.ftc.gov/bcp/conline/pubs/online/cybrsmrt.htm* and the American Bar Association's Web site at *www.safeshopping.org*.

Next, can you generate some innovative, not-yet-published ideas based on your experiences as shoppers and also business employees? Use the quality-to-security tools—brainstorming and cause-and-effect analysis—to generate some unique ideas for safe and secure cybershopping. In the next step, peruse your own company's Web site.

Step 2. Visit your own company's Web site. Does it meet all of the above criteria? Be sure your company practices what it preaches. Recommend any necessary modifications be made before continuing to the next exercise.

Exercise 2. Create Letters to the Consumer

Estimated Time: Four Hours

It is time to brag about your safe and secure company. Using the e-shopping best practices list from exercise 1 together with details on the security standards your company provides for its customers and employees, create a series of *one-paragraph* letters to the consumer, for use in a series of newspaper advertisements, and meet with management to develop a time plan to integrate these letters into the company's broad e-business marketing plan.

Step 1. Divide the team into groups and work together to create 10 letters—5 per team. The guidelines for the format of the letters are:

- Each letter is to be no more than one paragraph in length and consist of no more than five short sentences.
- Each letter is to be complete with date, salutation (to our customers and employees), and signature (company chief executive officer).
- Each letter is to follow from the previous letter, so that the letters can be published sequentially.

There are two guidelines for the content of each letter:

1. In three to four sentences, tell a short story about how your company protects its people (hint: think about a Security Standard).
2. In one to two sentences, give customers a helpful tip or two for safe cybershopping.

When creating these one-paragraph letters, incorporate the term "identity theft." After all, that is what this is all about

Step 2. Now implement the plan. Working as a team, discuss, decide, and set a calendar—time, date, and place—for unrolling the series of letters.

Then meet with management to propose and integrate the plan into the existing marketing program.

Exercise 3. Create a Web Page

Estimated Time: Three Hours

The project team now has all the necessary content material to design a creative Web page titled "E-Commerce Best Practices for Our Customers." To create this page, work together as a team using the items generated in exercise 1 together with the brief paragraphs created in exercise 2. Create a "clean" and easy-to-read page for current and potential customers by interspersing the brief paragraphs on how your company employs the BISP Security Standards for their protection. For emphasis, use bullet points for items that provide tips for safe e-shopping.

In summary, the project team, and your company, has gone beyond the competition in two important ways. First, you have proactively confronted identity theft by promoting the security standards for prevention, and, second, your open letters to *consumers* and the Web page for *customers* communicate the positive message that consumers wish to hear: *Your company cares.* Monitoring identity theft continues in the next chapter with legislative controls that prevent identity theft but that do not jeopardize a company's budget or operations.

CHAPTER 22

THE LEGISLATIVE PROCESS

Financial and other institutions must take a stand on identity theft legislation before others take a stand against them. That is, some legislation could be enacted that would require cost prohibitive measures for compliance that, for some companies, could jeopardize the ability to compete and contribute to the overall economy of the United States.

Unfortunately, legislation is not always based on firsthand information. Financial institutions, which are closer to the identity theft problem, and other businesses are in positions of authority when it comes to identity theft legislation. Further, employees of those businesses are in the best position of all to influence enactment of cost-effective and preventive legislation that will not simultaneously impede the firms' ability to do business. This chapter discusses identity theft on the legislative front.

STANDARD 16. IDENTITY THEFT LEGISLATIVE PROCESS

Goals: Design, propose, and prepare a press release announcing proactive legislation in identity theft prevention.

Specific Objectives: The majority of legislation on identity theft is reactive; that is, legislation enacted as a reaction to a crime already committed.

Examples abound in numerous laws passed in the name of consumer protection. Reactive legislative is important. More important, however, is legislation that proactively prevents identity crimes from occurring in the first place.

At the same time, lawmakers who propose such laws may be unaware that many bills could potentially restrict business practices—the laws may require expensive methods for prevention or in other ways interfere with, or go beyond, a company's financial capability.

Business has the best perspective from which to craft identity theft legislation. The objectives for Standard 16 therefore are to design *preventive* legislation that also *is not prohibitively restrictive.*

Orientation

To take a stand on identity theft legislation, the project team must, first, be aware of already enacted and proposed legislation. In preparation for completing Standard 16, carefully read the descriptions of federal and state legislation that has been enacted and proposed, beginning with the Identity Theft Act of 1998.[1]

Federal legislation makes the theft or criminal use of personal information a crime through the enactment of the Identity Theft and Assumption Deterrence Act of 1998 (Public Law 105-318). The act criminalizes fraud in connection with the unlawful theft and misuse of personal identifying information (i.e., name; address; mother's maiden name; and Social Security, driver's license, credit card, and other financial account numbers). A previous provision (Section 1028) dealt only with the transfer of personal information as it appears or is used in documents. The 1998 act amended now toughens the penalty provisions of Section 1028. With some exceptions, violators are generally subject to a fine and/or imprisonment of up to 15 years.

Section 3 of the act amends 18 United States Code Section 1028 by, among other things, adding a new subsection to establish an offense by anyone who "knowingly transfers or uses, without lawful authority, a means of identification of another person with the intent to commit, or to aid or abet, any unlawful activity that constitutes a violation of Federal law, or that constitutes a felony under any applicable State or local law."

"Means of identification" has been amended to include "any name or number that may be used, alone or in conjunction with any other information, to identify a specific individual." Specific examples include an individual's name; Social Security number; date of birth; driver's license; unique biometric data, such as fingerprints or iris image; and unique electronic identification number and telecommunication identifying information or access device, such as an access code or personal identification number.

Since the 1998 Act and in response to an explosion in identity theft crimes in California, lawmakers in that state have led the way in identity theft legislation. For example, U.S. Senator Dianne Feinstein proposed legislation for speedier prosecution and tougher prison sentences for thieves who steal identities and use them to create fraudulent driver's licenses, credit cards, passports, and other identifying documents. California also has many other proposals under review (or already enacted) that can be used as models for business-proposed legislation in other states. However, implementing and enforcing some proposed legislation may be cost prohibitive, especially for smaller companies.

Step 1. As a team, and in preparation for recommending legislation, review some laws enacted or proposed. Consider how some of the existing bills from other states may be useful in your state and for your company. Consider as well how some of those bills may serve to either impede or promote a company's financial ability to compete. Knowledge of current federal and state laws may also trigger ideas for their amendments for extensions or other modifications, or for new laws that would serve your company (and society) by helping to foster a corporate environment of both security and economic growth. From these perspectives, therefore, read and discuss as a team the following summary statements from Senate Bills (SB) and Assembly Bills (AB):

- *Senate Bill 125, Alpert*: Requires credit card companies, financial organizations, lenders, and consumer utility companies to give identity theft victims information about attempts to use their identities.

- *Senate Bill 168, Bowen*: Prohibits any business or government agency from printing an individual's Social Security number on any card required for the individual to access products or services.
- *Senate Bill 168, Bowen*: Prohibits printing an individual's Social Security number on any materials that are mailed to the individual, unless required by state or federal law.
- *Senate Bill 222, Torlakson*: Requires the Office of Criminal Justice Planning to establish regional identity theft units. The units would investigate and prosecute identity theft suspects, conduct a public awareness campaign about identity theft, and act as regional information clearinghouses for victims, law enforcement, and media.
- *Senate Bill 661, Dunn*: Requires the Department of Motor Vehicles (DMV) to create a biometric identifier from a driver's license applicant's thumbprint or fingerprint and ensure that each individual is issued only one driver's license or identification card. The bill would prohibit the department from providing any information collected under these provisions to a third party.
- *Senate Bill 766, Karnette*: Requires a person requesting a duplicate driver's license to apply in person. The bill would require the Department of Motor Vehicles to compare all photographs and information on file to the likeness and information obtained from a person requesting the duplicate.
- *Assembly Bill 468, Cohn*: Requires a person who is requesting a duplicate driver's license or identity card to provide photographic proof of identity.
- *Senate Bill 1050, Torlakson*: Requires the Department of Consumer Affairs to report to the legislature on a system to permit retailers to verify identification when a customer uses a check or credit card, and on a system to ensure that businesses comply with the law that prohibits printing more than the last five digits of a credit card number on receipts.

- *Assembly Bill 60, Cedillo*: Requires every driver's license application to contain the applicant's Social Security number, but specifies that it shall not be included on any driver's license, identification card, registration, certificate of title, or any other DMV document.
- *Assembly Bill 245, Wyland*: Redefines the crime of identity theft to eliminate the requirement that the prosecutor must prove that a perpetrator obtained the victim's identifying information without authorization.
- *Assembly Bill 371, Koretz*: Requires a consumer credit-reporting agency to notify a consumer when the agency has received five credit inquiries in a 60-day period or has received a report that would add negative information to the consumer's file. The reporting agency then would be required to give the consumer a free copy of his or her file on request.
- *Assembly Bill 488, Kehoe*: Gives a consumer the right to request and receive a record of all inquiries to a consumer credit reporting agency resulting in the provision of information about the consumer in the year preceding the consumer's request, and would require a consumer credit reporting agency to disclose, upon request of the consumer, the credit inquirers' customer service addresses and telephone numbers.
- *Assembly Bill 655, Wright*: Allows a consumer to request his or her name be removed from lists that a consumer credit reporting agency furnishes for credit card solicitations, and would require the agency to inform a consumer of this.
- *Assembly Bill 1155, Dutra*: Makes it a felony-misdemeanor for a government employee, as part of an identity theft criminal conspiracy, to give a driver's license, identification card, vehicle registration, or other DMV document to a person who is not entitled to the document.
- *Assembly Bill 1289, Florez*: Prohibits a financial institution from disclosing or making an unrelated use of a consumer's personal information without the consumer's prior written consent The bill also would prohibit a business, private organization, or state or

local agency from using a person's Social Security number to identify the person as an employee or client.

- *Assembly Bill 1474, Briggs*: Requires the DMV to create a fingerprint identification system to be funded from the fees charged for
driver's licenses and identification cards.

In addition to the above proposed or enacted legislation, U.S. Senators
Dianne Feinstein (D-Calif.), Jon Kyl (R-Ariz.), and Chuck Grassley
(R-Iowa) have introduced legislation that would require credit bureaus to
inform a consumer if someone applied for a credit card in their name
from an address other than the one the bureaus have on file.

Other legislation proposed by U.S. Senator Maria Cantwell (D-Wash.)
would allow consumers to obtain copies of credit card applications and
bills in their names. The Cantwell bill also includes provisions designed
to make it easier for consumers to undo the damage caused by identity
thieves.

Appendix K presents a list of legislators and others who first came out
in support of identity theft measures, who have been victims of the crime,
and/or who have testified before or sit on various committees dealing either
directly or indirectly with identity thefts. Since it was created, this list has
expanded to include many others across the country who have pursued or
are actively pursuing legislation to combat identity theft. Not all of this legislation may be practical from a company's financial perspective.

The challenge for the project team in the exercises that follow is to
generate a list of best possible legislative proposals for the prevention of
identity theft, as a way to advocate for your business customers and also
enable your company to profit financially.

Exercise 1. Review the Identity Theft Laws

Estimated Time: Four Hours
To begin, and before developing your company's customer advocate
proposals for identity theft legislation, review the federal and state identity theft laws that are enacted or currently proposed.

Step 1. Obtain four lists of identity theft legislation, two federal and two state. These lists cover:

1. Enacted federal legislation
2. Proposed federal legislation
3. Enacted legislation in your state
4. Proposed legislation in your state

Obtain these lists from the federal government Web site and from your state government Web site. For information on federal legislation, go to *www.whitehouse.gov/government/legi.html* and follow the links to the House of Representatives and the Senate. For information on state legislation, go to www.[abbreviatednameofstate].gov: for example: *www.mi.gov* for the State of Michigan Web site, or *www.mn.gov* for the State of Minnesota Web site.

Step 2. Review and discuss as a team the federal and state legislation that has been proposed or enacted. To narrow the lists, briefly discuss and then place a checkmark by only those acts or bills that stand out as potentially *non*detrimental, from a business perspective. That is, for each law, pose these questions:

- Does it require resources for company compliance?
- Is such compliance feasible for small companies with limited resources?
- Does it require large investments of a company's time?
- Does it require reorganizing, restructuring, or otherwise redesigning *your* company's current business practices or procedures?

This list of legislation will be used together with *expert information* obtained in exercise 2 as the basis for proposing legislation to protect employees and their customers.

Exercise 2. Prepare to Develop Legislation

Estimated Time: Three Hours
The goal is to develop a list of company proposals for identity theft legislation *in your state* that are proactive, that would protect consumers

and businesses, and that can be reasonably implemented by businesses of any size. In preparation, it is necessary to conduct a focus group interview with a group of criminal justice professionals. Before beginning this exercise and to ensure the most productive outcomes, once again review the instructions in Appendix E for the Security Focus Group Interview.

This focus group interview is imperative because preventive legislation requires knowledge of measures that would help law enforcement to apprehend criminals and give attorneys the power to prosecute them. Identity theft is still considered a low-risk crime; few laws exist to help prevent it. For example, police departments do not have the resources to fight crimes that are not likely to be prosecuted, and legal jurisdictional boundaries interfere with the investigation and prosecution of identity theft networks, which, by criminal design, operate intentionally across legal jurisdictions. These and many other reasons for escalations in identity theft are known only by the experts who confront identity crimes on a daily basis.

Step 1. Extend the invitation. Set a date, prepare the agenda, and compose and send a formal letter of invitation to your city's police chief and to prosecutors from your state's attorney general's office to attend a two-hour focus group interview on legislation that would help those criminal justice professionals combat identity theft. Recall that a goal is to represent your company as a consumer advocate for identity theft protection. Such legislation, drafted and promoted by your company, would strongly convey the message you wish to send consumers.

Step 2. Conduct the two-hour focus group interview. Then consolidate and prepare the ideas generated from this interview for use in exercise 3, where the project team is to create legislation for your own state.

Exercise 3. Develop Legislation on Identity Theft

Estimated Time: Four Hours
Use the list of federal and state laws checkmarked in exercise 1 and the list of ideas generated from the criminal justice professionals in exercise

2 as the basis for formal brainstorming followed by cause-and-effect analysis. The goal is to generate several creative ideas that can be framed as proposals to proactively prevent the thefts of consumer identities.

Each proposal should address two questions:

1. Is the proposed legislation proactive, that is, will it help to mitigate or prevent identity thefts?
2. From the perspectives of team members, is the proposal a wise business practice, that is, one that will not financially inhibit businesses, regardless of size?

Proposals developed from these two perspectives may potentially benefit not only the consumer but other businesses as well, inasmuch as criminals do not discriminate as to which businesses to victimize.

To help guide the project team in this exercise, consider the proposals from exercise 1 as potential proposals that could be enacted in your state. Consider each proposal from the perspective of law enforcement and how a bill might be strengthened with a law enforcement practice, based on the focus group interview. Using brainstorming, try to generate new ideas not previously proposed—laws that would not require financial investments for the way a company does business. Seek also to create proposals that will convey to the public the message that your company is a consumer advocate for identity theft protection. These results will be used in exercise 4 for presentations to the state legislature.

Exercise 4. Present Proposals and Issue Press Release

Estimated Time: Four Hours

As a final exercise, make follow-through plans with specific target dates to formally present your package of identity theft proposals to your state's legislature, and issue a press release to make it known that your company is an advocate for customer security.

Finally, Chapter 23 is a brief summary for healthcare and healthcare-related companies that assume an enormous responsibility for securing hundreds of thousands of personal identities contained in the Health Insurance Portability and Accountability Act database. The chapter illustrates how easy it is for these companies to fully comply with federal laws for securing personal information in this database.

CHAPTER 23

THE HIPAA DATABASE

When it became effective in 2003, the Health Insurance Portability and Accountability Act (HIPAA) of 1998[1] provided criminals with thousands of new opportunities to steal personal information. How? The HIPAA created a database containing the identifying information on nearly everyone in the United States — all persons who either have healthcare insurance or who have in the past received healthcare.

However, healthcare or healthcare-related institutions need not worry provided they have secured the HIPAA database on the four fronts: people, processes, property, and (thereby) proprietary information. The security standards of the Business Information Security Program (BISP) are essential compliance requirements for all institutions having access to the HIPAA database. This chapter presents an overview of preceding chapters so as to illustrate the BISP applications for businesses providing healthcare services and products.

THE BISP SECURITY STANDARDS AND HIPAA

Goal: To prevent the theft of personal identifying information from the HIPAA database.

Specific Objectives: The objectives of this chapter are twofold: (1) to provide healthcare and healthcare-related companies with a brief overview of the BISP security standards contained in Parts II and III, and

(2) to summarize sections of the chapters describing how personal information can be compromised from institutions having access to the HIPAA database.

Orientation

Although all U.S. health insurance companies, hospitals, clinics, pharmacies, home health agencies, clinical laboratories, medical supply stores, nursing homes, billing services, and assorted clinics and centers by now are presumably aware of their legal responsibility for preventing identity theft, personal identities cannot be secured without implementing the Security Standards that protect three fronts: people, processes, and property.

On the *people front*, for example, the Gramm-Leach-Bliley Act (GLB Act) recommends reference checks of employees prior to hiring. This is a troublesome recommendation to businesses for at least two reasons.

1. Businesses that provide third parties with personal information about previous employees put themselves in jeopardy for lawsuits by those employees.
2. Libraries are filled with volumes of applied management research showing how reference checks lack validity and reliability when used for personnel selection purposes. Reference checks simply do not work.

Additionally, on the *process front*, neither the GLB nor any other act addresses the security of information processes — those sequential job tasks (i.e., the process) that, to perform the job, require access to personal identifying information.

Consider, for example, the multiple job tasks that use personal information from a healthcare form provided by a patient who comes into a dental office. The patient's personal identifiers are directly accessible by as many as five people: receptionist, nurse, dentist, billing company, and most or all other office personnel.

As earlier chapters fully recognized, federal safeguards are required to address computer and network system security. But as was also mentioned earlier, *computers do not steal identities*. Machine security is only one aspect of identity theft prevention, and a relatively small one at that. The security of the *people* who have access to the computers is of the most immediate importance, followed by *process* security and then *property* security — the security of the computer and network systems.

The compromising of personal information from computer systems can be largely mitigated and even prevented by securing first the people and then the processes that use the personal information. Computer security is only a patch to cover up the root causes: the lack of people and process security.

The security problems for healthcare and related businesses due to the accessibility of the HIPAA database by hundreds of thousands of companies and their employees is unfortunate because the act provides important protections for millions of working Americans and their families who have preexisting medical conditions or might suffer discrimination in health coverage based on a factor that relates to an individual's health.

For example, the act:

- Limits exclusions for preexisting conditions
- Prohibits discrimination against employees and dependents based on their health status
- Guarantees renewability and availability of health coverage to certain employers and individuals
- Protects many workers who lose health coverage by providing better access to individual health insurance coverage.

But it seems that these many blessings for U.S. citizens are incidental to HIPAA's real purpose.

HIPAA's Real Purpose

The Proposed Rule for the National Standard Health Care Provider Identifier that is used in the HIPAA national database was reported in volume 63, number 88, of the *Federal Register* on Thursday, May 7,

1998. The Proposed Rule was published by the Department of Health and Human Services in the section titled "National Standards" and the subsection titled "Identifier Standards."[2]

Accordingly, "the 'Rule' proposes a standard for a national health care provider identifier. *The purpose of HIPAA and the Rule is for faster, electronic processing of financial and administrative transactions*" (emphasis added). Based on this report by the U.S. Department of Health and Human Services, the primary purpose for HIPAA is economical — quicker claims processing for healthcare providers. The healthcare provisions for citizens are a secondary by-product. And given the lack of security, citizens may be hindered rather than helped by HIPAA. The contents of the database are unbelievable.

Contents of the HIPAA "National Identity" Database

Instead of being helped by HIPAA, thousands of citizens may suffer from the costs and stresses of identity theft, because the provisions in the act for securing their personal information are limited and lacking, and the databases contain life history information on many or most U.S. citizens. The following examples represent only a part of a longer list of personal information available in the database: patient's name, address, birth date, birthplace, citizenship, gender, race, maiden name, marital name, middle name, Social Security number, place of employment; past, present, and future physical and mental healthcare services and all details for each health-related incident, including admission and discharge date, weight, diagnosis, treatment, medications; also date of future scheduled surgery and all other information requested by a healthcare provider for healthcare and insurance purposes (p. 25320). The HIPAA database also contains the same health information on spouses and dependents (p. 25320).

Furthermore, the term "health information" means any information, whether oral or recorded in any form or medium that is created or received by a health plan, public health authority, employer, life insurer, school or university, healthcare clearinghouse, home health agency, hospice, hospital, specialty outpatient, pharmacy, medical lab, dental lab, physician, osteopath, dentist, podiatrist, chiropractor, ophthalmologist, optometrist, and any other healthcare professional (pp. 25320; 25335–338).

In addition, the database also holds information on health claims, health encounters, health claims attachments, health plan enrollments, health plan disenrollments, health plan eligibility, healthcare payments and remittances, health plan premium payments, first reports of injury, health claim status, referral certifications and authorizations . . . and any other financial and administrative transactions that are determined to be appropriate" (p. 25322).

The greatest concern from an information security management perspective is the thousands or millions of people who now have access to the database and background information on U.S. citizens. One recent estimate is that as much as one-third of identity thefts come out of healthcare facilities, and this study was conducted *before* the enactment of HIPAA and the creation of its national identity database.[3]

The predicted surge in identity thefts also can be blamed in great part on the accessiblity given to the hundreds (potentially thousands) of other organizations that also have access to the database, such as "repricing companies, community health management information systems, value-added networks, software system vendors, *and other second- and third-party claims processors and clearinghouses*" (emphasis added).[3] To ignore the probability that identity thefts will increase due to HIPAA shows great disregard for American citizens, given the recent history and astonishing increase in identity theft crimes.

However, those healthcare and related companies that take the time — recall, the cost is negligible — to adopt the Business Information Security Program's standards can demonstrate their concern by securing *within their own institutions* the personal identifying information of their employees and that of their patients, clients, and other customers.

Examples of the BISP Security Standard Exercises

The security standards are developed by teams of employees through a series of step-by-step and detailed instructions with representative illustrations and examples of both the procedures and the standards themselves. The tangible documents prove that security mechanisms have been developed and implemented. The exercises use proven tools and procedures from industrial and organizational psychology, the management sciences, and the field of criminal justice to secure people, processes, and property and, thereby, proprietary information — personal identifiers.

To illustrate, the next three exercises are summary examples from chapters in this book that provide step-by-step instructions for developing security standards to secure work *processes* in three steps: (1) identify, (2) trace, and (3) secure.

Exercise 1

Identify HIPAA incoming sources. Use structured brainstorming (Appendix C) to determine where the HIPAA information (identities of your employees and customers) enters into or originates within a department. To perform this exercise, generate a list of all incoming sources, or entry points, of identities into the department. Focus on places where information first enters a department or where information (identities) is generated within a department (e.g., receptionist desk). Perform this exercise for each department that either directly or indirectly has access to the HIPAA database.

Exercise 2

Trace the identifying information, that is, the form or document that contains the personal information (e.g., an application for healthcare or healthcare insurance). Start the tracing where the HIPAA document comes into a department (exercise 1) to trace the *process* — the input-throughput-output flow of the identity through the department. Use the specific procedures and detailed instructions to trace *how* and *where* the information is processed through a department. For example:

how refers to → distribute → deliver → sort

where refers to → desk → mailbox → computer

Use the described universal engineering symbols to label the paths that HIPAA information takes as it flows (is processed through sequentially performed job tasks and job positions) through a department. Build on the flow chart by conducting structured and formal brainstorming and using cause-and-effect analysis and the four M's: manpower, methods, machine, and materials.

Exercise 3

Secure the HIPAA process. Use the results from the formal brainstorming and the cause-and-effect analysis (and other methods described within the chapters) to generate mechanisms to secure the work processes.

Exercise 4

Develop short- and long-term strategic plans to implement these security mechanisms. Short-term plans are those that can be put into effect immediately without much cost or time. Long-term plans require formal approval and possibly budgeting. Be specific with target dates.

In summary, these four brief examples describe the straightforward and easy-to-use methods that are universally established and widely documented for their effectiveness in producing results that are valid and reliable. These are the methods used in this book to help companies provide comprehensive security for employees and customers.

Healthcare companies have come under harsh public scrutiny because of the costs of healthcare. Now, due to the increasing public awareness of the HIPAA database, consumers are even more fearful and hesitant when seeking services or products from healthcare businesses. This is unfortunate because there really is no cause for concern when a company has secured its business border inclusively and exhaustively, going beyond computer security. Companies that institute the BISP security standards will be in full compliance with federal laws and while doing so can also become recognized as concerned advocates for consumer security.

Now, it is time to congratulate the two project teams and company employees who helped build security for your company!

CONGRATULATIONS
TO
THE PROJECT TEAMS!

YOUR COMPANY
INFORMATION SECURITY
CERTIFIED
APRIL 2005

You can be proud that each member of your project team is directly responsible for the information security in your company. You and your coworkers and customers now can be confident that by maintaining and enforcing the 22 Security Standards, your company's borders are secured on all four fronts: people, processes, property, and proprietary information.

I look forward with anticipation to the Annual Awards Ceremony to personally present your team with the distinguished Business Information Security Programs (BISP) "Seal of Information Security"

Judith M. Collins, Ph.D. and Director
Michigan State University
Business Identity
Theft Partnerships in Prevention
www.cj.msu.edu/~outreach/identity
idtheft@msu.edu

APPENDICES

THE SECURITY STANDARD CHECKLIST

IDENTITY THEFT PREVENTION

Project Team #1

Security Standard 1 (Chapter 8): Identify Identities

Exercise 1.   _____Identify "personal" identities

Exercise 2.   _____Organize "personal" identities and determine entry points

Exercise 3.   _____Identify "business" identities

Exercise 4.   _____Organize "business" identities and determine entry points

Security Standard 2 (Chapter 8): Match Identities

Exercise 1.   _____Determine "internal" job titles

Exercise 2.   _____Match "internal" job titles with "personal" and "business" identities

Exercise 3.   _____Determine "external" job titles

Exercise 4.   _____Match "external" job titles with "personal" and "business" identities

Security Standard 3 (Chapter 9): The Security Job Analysis
Exercise 1.   _____Identify job tasks
Exercise 2.   _____Create checklist of job tasks
Exercise 3.   _____Administer checklist to incumbent-experts
Exercise 4.   _____Score checklist
Exercise 5.   _____The security job description

Security Standard 4 (Chapter 10): Recruitment for Security
Exercise 1.   _____"Snowballing"
Exercise 2.   _____Involve current employees
Exercise 3.   _____Solicit new applicants
Exercise 4.   _____Use personnel agencies

Security Standard 5 (Chapter 11): Personnel Selection for Security
Exercise 1.   _____The Cognitive Ability Test: Option A
Exercise 2.   _____The Cognitive Ability Test: Option B

Security Standard 6 (Chapter 12): Select for Motivation
Exercise 1.   _____The Motivation Test: Option A
Exercise 2.   _____The Motivation Test: Option B

Security Standard 7 (Chapter 13): Select for Integrity and Security
Exercise 1.   _____The Integrity for Security Test: Option A
Exercise 2.   _____The Integrity for Security Test: Option B

Security Standard 8 (Chapter 14): Select for Interpersonal Skills
Exercise 1.   _____The Test of Interpersonal Skills: Option A
Exercise 2.   _____The Test of Interpersonal Skills: Option B

Security Standard 9 (Chapter 15): Socialization, Company Culture, Realistic Job Preview
Exercise 1.   _____Assess company culture
Exercise 2.   _____Further analyze to identify improvements

Exercise 3.   _____Create realistic job preview
Exercise 4.   _____Develop strategic plans

Security Standard 10 (Chapter 16): The Security Orientation Program

Exercise 1.   _____Design security orientation program
Exercise 2.   _____Prepare written agenda for orientation program
Exercise 3.   _____Present security orientation program to current employees

Security Standard 11 (Chapter 17): The Appraisal and Feedback Instrument

Exercise 1.   _____Develop individual appraisal instrument
Exercise 2.   _____Develop group appraisal instrument
Exercise 3.   _____Develop self-appraisal instrument
Exercise 4.   _____Develop departmental appraisal instrument
Exercise 5.   _____Develop time plans and procedures
Exercise 6.   _____Recognize and reward employees

Project Team #2

Security Standard 12 (Chapter 18): Secure Information Processes

Step 1.   _____Carefully review Chapter 6
Step 2.   _____Create project team
Step 3.   _____The quality-to-security tools: Overview
Step 4.   _____Brainstorming
Step 5.   _____Cause-and-effect analysis
Step 6.   _____Flow chart analysis
Step 7.   _____Pareto analysis
Exercise 1.   _____Identify sources of personal identities
Exercise 2.   _____Track the flow of personal identities
Exercise 3.   _____Locate weaknesses in information processes
Exercise 4.   _____Prioritize weaknesses in processes

Exercise 5.   _____Secure information processes
Exercise 6.   _____Develop time plan

Security Standard 13 (Chapter 19): The E-Business Web Site

Exercise 1.   _____Develop web site security assessment
Exercise 2.   _____The web site security assessment: Administer, score,
                   interpret

Security Standard 14 (Chapter 20): The Customer Security Program Document

Step 1.   _____Listen to victim
Step 2.   _____Review "Process of Healing" exercises with victim
Step 3.   _____Instruct victim on immediate steps
Step 4.   _____Discuss with victim the "Process of Healing"
Step 5.   _____Instruct victim on additional steps
Step 6.   _____Inform victim of credit report reviews
Step 7.   _____Advise victims on writing letters of correction
Step 8.   _____Advise victims of the police assistance role

Security Standard 15 (Chapter 21): E-Commerce "Best Practices" for Customers

Exercise 1.   _____Develop e-commerce best practices
Exercise 2.   _____Create letters to consumers
Exercise 3.   _____Create a web page

Security Standard 16 (Chapter 22): The Legislative Process

Exercise 1.   _____Review identity theft laws
Exercise 2.   _____Develop legislation on identity theft
Exercise 3.   _____Present proposals, issue press release

APPENDIX B

CHECKLIST OF TEAM PREREQUISITES

1. _____ Elect, select, or seek volunteer employees who will comprise the project team.
2. _____ Select a minimum of three and a maximum of five employees for team membership.
3. _____ Include at least one manager from the department being secured.
4. _____ Select long-tenured employees, those most familiar with departmental jobs.
5. _____ Select team members able to meet consistently each week throughout the project.
6. _____ Choose team members from the same or interrelated departments.
7. _____ Choose as team members employees who hold different job positions within the department.

APPENDIX C

STRUCTURED AND FORMAL BRAINSTORMING: STEP-BY-STEP INSTRUCTIONS

The quality management literatures use a common definition with standardized instructions for conducting brainstorming, sometimes called "structured" or "formal" brainstorming. The following paraphrased definition and instructions are borrowed, in parts, from several different quality management authorities.[1]

DEFINITION OF FORMAL BRAINSTORMING

Brainstorming: (1) is a problem-solving method (2) used to generate ideas by (3) using the creative process of employees working together as a team (4) whereby each team member capitalizes on the synergy created by the group process, for the goal of (5) developing a large list of specific ideas.

Brainstorming is used to investigate, analyze, and identify causes and also solutions to problems. To be effective, brainstorming requires disciplined participation in a process that follows a particular structure, which the quality management literature refers to as "structured" and "formal."

The benefits of brainstorming are that a large list of ideas can be generated in a short time period by a team of members who are involved in this process. The process also promotes group participation, cohesion, and unity.

STEP-BY-STEP INSTRUCTIONS

Use these structured guidelines for your brainstorming session:

- Create a team, or teams, of three to five employees, including at least one manager. The ideal group size is five.
- Use a round or rectangular table so that each team member will face all others, an arrangement important for visual and direct communications.
- The team selects a recorder: someone who will later print the results of brainstorming.
- Use a large flip chart located near the table. At the top of the flip chart, clearly and concisely print a heading that briefly defines the team's task. Exhibit C.1 shows a formal brainstorming task statement taken from an actual exercise.
- Allow 10 to 15 minutes for "think" time. During this time, team members independently generate their own lists of ideas about solving the problem in the task statement. This is also "quiet" time during which there is to be no discussion.
- Members write each idea on a Post-it note, using one Post-it for each idea.
- After the personal think time, use the round robin approach to generate a larger number of ideas: Each person, one at a time around the table, states one idea from only one Post-it note. There is no discussion of ideas during the round robin listing of ideas: This is the "discipline" required of structured and formal brainstorming.

- As each person states an idea, the recorder *numbers* and then *clearly prints* this idea on the flip chart. The team will be working from this list.
- As the round robin proceeds, each team member jots down on a *new* Post-it note any new ideas that are triggered as others state their ideas. This is called the "idea generating" phase and the synergy of brainstorming.
- Permit no evaluation of ideas during the round robin. The round robin is the team's think time.
- Give everyone an equal chance to participate, in turn.
- Pass when you have used up your Post-it notes of ideas.
- The recorder continues to keep the ideas visible by using the large flip chart sheets.
- When all team members have "passed," the round robin is completed.

Now it's time to discuss. Follow these guidelines for discussion:

- Make sure that everyone understands each item on the list.
- Be clear and specific about each item.
- Eliminate duplicate items.
- Combine similar or common items.

To summarize, the structured rules for disciplined and formal brainstorming are:

- Start with 10 to 15 minutes of "think" time.
- Contribute in turn.
- Allow one idea per person per turn.
- You may pass.
- Do not explain ideas.
- Do not criticize others' ideas.
- Aim for quantity.

EXHIBIT C.1   *A Brainstorming Task Statement*

The following statement was taken from the heading of a flip chart used in an actual brainstorming session. Notice that the statement spells out precisely the task to be performed.

"Determine the Factors to Be Included in a Bioterrorism Contingency Plan for the University Auditorium."

EXHIBIT C.2   *A Brainstorming List*

Taken from an actual case, the task statement was:

"Determine All Sources of Personal Identities Coming into the Automobile Leasing Department."

The following list was created from this task statement:

1. Phone
2. E-mail
3. U.S. mail
4. Interoffice mail
5. In-person application

APPENDIX D

CAUSE-AND-EFFECT ANALYSIS: STEP-BY-STEP INSTRUCTIONS

Cause-and-effect analysis builds on and organizes the ideas gener-ated in brainstorming. The Business Information Security Program (BISP) adapts the cause-and-effect analysis method from the manage-ment sciences to organize the list of identities generated in brainstorm-ing sessions.

Cause-and-effect analysis uses the quality management fishbone framework.

According to this quality management theory, the source of all man-agement problems can be attributed to four Ms: manpower, methods, machine, and materials.

In the context of the BISP model, *manpower* refers to people; *meth-ods* are the work processes, policies, or procedures; the *machines* refer to all types of equipment and represents property; and *material* also may be property, in the form of documents, application forms, and any other products used to perform the job tasks.

As an example, exercises in Chapter 8 identify the incoming sources of identities into a department. If documents containing personal information are hand delivered, "hand delivery" would be a source categorized under manpower, and if personal information is also delivered through a phone conversation, the source term "telephone" would be categorized and listed under the heading "machines," and so on.

The cause-and-effect fishbone four-M framework is used throughout for problem-solving exercises. The items shown on the fishbones in Exhibits D.1 and D.2 were borrowed from the flip chart of one company (where identities were stolen) to illustrate how an item can be categorized under each of the four Ms. For this particular exercise, the team was determining "why" identities might have been stolen from the department. The team's task statement was, simply, "Why Identities Are Stolen."

EXHIBIT D.1 *Cause-and-Effect Analysis for Incoming Identities*

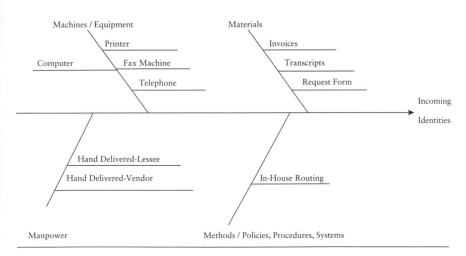

Note: Item examples on fishbone frame selected from an actual company where identities had been stolen.

EXHIBIT **D.2**   *Cause-and-Effect Analysis of Sources of SSN Thefts*

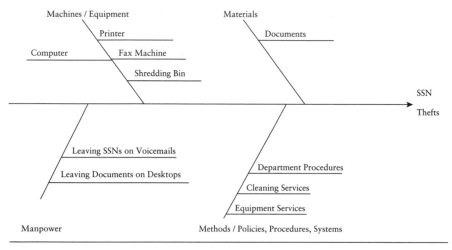

Note: SSNs refer to Social Security numbers; several items selected from an actual case.

THE SECURITY FOCUS GROUP INTERVIEW

Some of the exercises in these chapters may benefit from information known to departmental employees who are not members of the employee-manager team. A focus "group" interview is ideal for generating such information because focus interviews are semistructured and efficient, and several employees can participate at one time. Focus group interviews are idea-generating processes used typically to gather information from customers about the design or utility of a product or service. For identity security, the Business Information Security Program adapts and employs the focus group interview for use with employees to elicit information about which job tasks might require knowledge of or have access to personal identities.

A job's title may suggest the job is a position of security, but job titles do not fully describe jobs. The focus group interview involves several employees in the same department and where work processes may be interrelated. Together, these individuals help to identify job positions that may frequently or infrequently use personal identities. *Throughout, the center of attention is on the job and not the person who holds the job—it is the job's process that is to be secured.*

Focus group interviews, like brainstorming, follow a formal structure and also build on the synergy of group members. Use these instructions to conduct the focus group interview.

- Elect a team member who will serve as the "moderator." The moderator's task is to keep the focus on the goal: to generate information about jobs within the department that use personal identities.
- Elect a second team member to record responses.
- As a team, identify and invite up to eight other *randomly selected* employees to participate in the focus group interview. Select these employees from different ranks and job positions to obtain information on a cross section of jobs.
- Arrange the table seating so that the employees and team members face one another.
- The moderator directs the discussion, but neither the moderator nor the team members express their views or make judgments about a job.
- The team is to emphasize that the focus is on the job and not the person who holds the job; it is the "job process" that eventually is to be secured, using the information elicited in this group interview.
- The moderator may use the following open-ended questions:
  - "What is the job's specific purpose?"
  - "Is personal information required to perform the job?"
  - "What types of personal information are used to perform job tasks?"
- Encourage participation by all focus group employees.
- The recorder uses a flip chart to list job positions as identified by the focus group members.
- Conduct the focus group interview in one hour or less.

THE SECURITY JOB DESCRIPTION

THE INFORMATION SECURITY RESEARCH INSTITUTE, LLC

Job Title	**COMPUTER FORENSIC ANALYST**
Department	Business Information Security
Reports To	Director
Grade	10
Exempt	___Yes ___No
Pay Range	12
Date	December 18, 2004

THIS JOB POSITION IS SECURITY-SENSITIVE _____YES _____NO

Purpose of the Job

Describe why this job exists.

Plan, coordinate, and implement security measures for the Business Information Security Program's four assets—(1) people, (2) processes, (3) proprietary information, and (4) property—to prevent unauthorized access, modification, destruction, theft, and disclosure of employee, customer, or business identifying information.

Essential Functions

List the essential duties required for this job as identified in the job analysis.

- Secure computer databases.
- Detect security intrusions.
- Perform process risk assessments.
- Analyze security requirements.
- Regulate access to proprietary information.
- Monitor use of information files.

Security-Related Essential Functions

- Secure computer databases.
- Detect security intrusions.
- Regulate access to proprietary information.
- Monitor use of information files.

Other Duties

What other important duties are performed occasionally, as identified in the job analysis?
- Conceal confidential information using encryption technology.
- Modify security procedures to incorporate new methods.
- Review violations of security procedures.
- Coordinate the Business Information Security Program with outside vendors.

THE SECURITY JOB DESCRIPTION

Knowledge, Skills, and Abilities

List the knowledge, skills, and abilities identified in the job analysis and any licenses or certifications required to perform the job tasks.

- Computer hardware and software certification: knowledge of circuit boards, processors, chips, electronic equipment, and hardware and software applications
- Knowledge of identity theft and identity crimes, and network modus operandi
- Knowledge of relevant security equipment and strategies to protect people, processes, proprietary information, and property
- Ability to communicate effectively
- Ability to analyze security requirements
- Ability to install security programs to meet specifications
- Ability to determine what kinds of equipment are needed for security
- Knowledge of quality management problem-solving tools
- Knowledge of information process risk assessment procedures
- Knowledge of personnel selection for security practices

Work Context

Here describe the working conditions of the job.
This job requires working indoors in environmentally controlled conditions; requires sitting, standing, and reaching and the use of hands to handle and control tools and equipment. The job requires the worker to coordinate or lead others in implementing security precautions and safeguards. The job tasks require high accuracy and exactness and the confidentiality of security-integrated mechanisms.

Work Values

What work values are required for this job?
The job position requires *honesty, trustworthiness, confidentiality, interpersonal skills, and self-motivated initiative* to perform independent or team-related job tasks that involve confidential personal and business identifying information. This job is results-oriented and allows employees to use their strongest abilities, giving them a feeling of *achievement*.

INDUSTRIAL AND ORGANIZATIONAL SPECIALISTS IN TEST DEVELOPMENT AND VALIDATION

Dr. Herman Aquinis
University of Colorado Business School
CB 165
PO Box 173364
Denver, Colorado 80217-3364

Dr. José Cortina
George Mason University
MSN 3F5
4400 University Drive
Fairfax, VA 22030-1182

Drs. Joyce & Robert Hogan
Hogan Assessment Systems
2622 E. 21st Street
Tulsa, OK 74114

Dr. Michael McDaniel
Virginia Commonwealth University
School of Business
12305 Collinstone Place
Glen Allen, VA 23059-7121

Dr. Paul Muchinsky
University of North Carolina—Greensboro
Business Administration
PO Box 26165
Greensboro, NC 27402-6165

Dr. Frank Schmidt
Tippie College of Business
University of Iowa
Iowa City, IA 52242

Dr. Neal Schmitt
Department of Psychology
Michigan State University
East Lansing, MI 48824-1117

Dr. Robert Tett
University of Tulsa
600 South College Avenue
Tulsa, OK 74104-3126

Dr. Judith Collins
School of Criminal Justice
Michigan State University
East Lansing, MI 48824-1118

ONE COMPANY'S SHORT- AND LONG-TERM STRATEGIC PLAN

The following example is a strategic plan developed by employees in one department of a large automobile manufacturing corporation. The team used the cause-and-effect analysis fishbone four-M model to identify the incoming sources into the department of both employee and customer Social Security numbers.

Strategic Timeline for Securing the Four M's

	Short versus Long Term	Target Date for Completion
Machines/Equipment		
1. Move printer to inner office.	short	immediate
2. Move fax to inner office.	short	immediate
3. Retrieve faxes when received.	short	immediate
4. Wait at fax until document has been sent.	short	immediate
5. Do not leave originals in fax machine.	short	immediate

	Short versus Long Term	*Target Date for Completion*
6. Lock computer screen when leaving desk.	short	immediate
7. Lock file cabinets at all times.	short	immediate
8. Make sure documents are shredded before walking away from shredder.	short	immediate

Materials

9. Produce only necessary documents.	short	immediate
10. Do not leave documents on desktop.	short	immediate

Methods

11. Do not leave identifying information on voice mail messages.	short	immediate
12. Change password often.	short	immediate

Manpower

13. Train all employees on above procedures.	short	week 1
14. Evaluate performance on above procedures.	short/long	month 1, 2 annual reviews

APPENDIX I

THE INFORMATION PROCESS: DEFINITION, DESCRIPTION, AND ILLUSTRATION

DEFINING THE INFORMATION PROCESS

Processes refer to the input-throughput-output of *information* that identifies employees or customers as this information is processed in a department, that is, the sequential job tasks processed while performing a job. Customer and employee *information*, or personal identities, are assets that can be secured by securing the information processes—the sequence of job tasks performed on the information (identities).

A process, for example, may be the sequence of tasks required to fill work orders or medical prescriptions, to conduct financial audits, to prepare employee payroll checks, to process credit card applications, or to open retail accounts for on-credit purchases. In each of these instances, the job tasks require names, addresses, Social Security numbers, and other personal information. Without these items of identifying information, there would be no job tasks to perform: The jobs exist to *process* them.

DESCRIBING AN *INFORMATION* PROCESS

This example (taken in part from Chapter 8) of an automobile leasing process is taken from an actual case in which corporate managers in a large automobile manufacturing plant lease automobiles for their own personal use. In this international corporation with hundreds of thousands of employees worldwide, as many as 100 or more of these and similar applications are processed daily.

The process begins when an application from a manager for the lease of an automobile comes into the leasing department through company mail, U.S. mail, e-mail, fax, or telephone; sometimes the application is personally hand delivered by the manager. The information on the application is then verified against company records to confirm that the applicant is indeed a company manager. A third step requires the verification of information (the identities) against the state's driver's license records to rule out disqualifying driving violations, which would stop the processing of the application. Subsequent job tasks related to the leasing of the auto are performed in different job positions. Finally, when all information is verified, the document continues to the last job tasks leading to the approval of the leased automobile to the manager.

Throughout the process, the identifying information of the manager seeking the automobile lease is handled in a series of sequentially ordered tasks linked to one another to form the work process. The application eventually is filed for renewal, and the process repeats, or discontinues—the name, Social Security number, and all other pieces of identifying information have been verified, acted on, and completed.

Throughout the many steps in this process, information can be compromised, either internally, by the relatively few dishonest employees who steal from the majority of upstanding employees and company customers, or externally, by company contractors, service providers, or others, such as, in the example, the state driver's license bureau. *However, information work processes can be secured.* To illustrate, the example continues (below) the case involving the automobile leasing department in which a team of managers and volunteer employees conducted an information process risk analysis. The solutions from this analysis were subsequently implemented and enforced by all of the employees in the leasing department.

ILLUSTRATING THE INFORMATION PROCESS RISK ASSESSMENT

Here is the background on how the team secured the leasing process. A manager wishing to lease an auto submits to the leasing department an application containing the following information: Social Security number (to verify employment), driver's license number (to verify driving record), date of birth (to verify the applicant), and home address (for verification and future correspondence). The manager submits the application to the leasing department through company mail, U.S. mail, e-mail, fax, telephone, or by personal delivery. The process itself—the sequence of job tasks—begins with the receipt of the application into the department. The information process risk assessment follows these job tasks.

Threats to security could come from each of the incoming sources. The manager-employee team first conducted brainstorming and cause-and-effect analysis to identify all of the potential incoming sources; they then used flow-charting to visually trace the flow of personal information through the department, following the job tasks—the standard, sequentially ordered tasks that are performed using the application. This flow of information can be thought of as the input-throughput-output of a document containing personal identities (or any other proprietary document, application, or other paper or digital form containing information). See Exhibit I.1 for common flow chart symbols. Exhibit I.2 shows the flow of information that routinely comes into the Leasing Department's Vehicle Inventory Unit. Note the key the team created to interpret the flow chart.

After the information process was visually charted, the project team analyzed each step in the process beginning at the point at which applications (information) arrive into the department. At each point on the flow chart, the team conducted brainstorming to generate all possible ways that identities could be comprised at that location or job position.

EXHIBIT I.1   *Common Flow Chart Symbols*

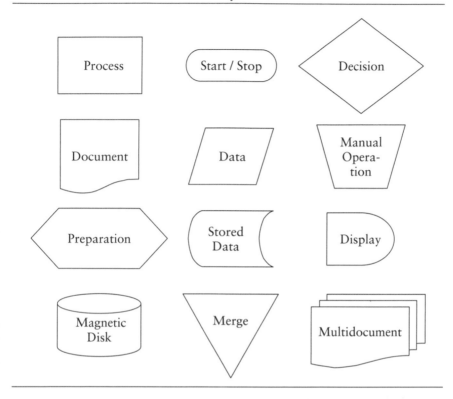

(Recall here the importance of maintaining the focus on the process, not the person performing the process.) The team was seeking to identify any possible weak linkages in the application process where an identity theft could occur. After the team members identified all possible susceptibilities to threat at each point in the information process, they again used brainstorming together with cause-and-effect analysis to generate a large number of options for management consideration to secure the weak points in the information process.

Here are some of the things the team recommended to management to secure the first point in the information process, the entry of information into the department. For the mailroom, the recommended security solutions were to (a) secure from passersby the otherwise relatively

EXHIBIT I.2   *Flow Chart Tracing the Route of a Fax Document through a*
Department—Each Location and Transfer Path Can Be Secured

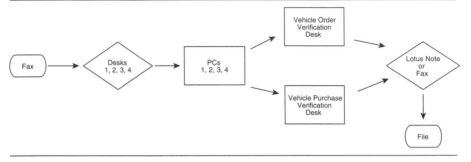

Source: Fax
Dept: Vehicle Inventory
Team Members: Frank, Martin, Janet, Marilyn, Peggy, Marlin
Desks:
   1 = Manager/Supervisor
   2 = CVMS Coordinator
   3 = D&B Coordinator
   4 = Authorization Code Coordinator

open mailroom by simply closing the door, (b) require the use of access
keys by departmental employees, (c) route (address) mail deliveries of
lease applications to specific mailboxes for (d) routine retrieval by specified job positions. These simple and inexpensive security precautions
served dual purposes: They tightened the perimeter of the mailroom,
thereby securing it from outside access, and they limited access to managers' identifying information to specific job positions of security.

Additionally, the fax machine was relocated to a more secure area,
and incoming fax applications were assigned to specific job positions
designated as position of security. E-mail lease applications were secured by simple policies to change the positions of desks or of computers on the desks, to protect the privacy of the screens showing
confidential information, and the usual computer security mechanisms
(e.g., virus protection, firewalls, spyware controls) were installed and
routinely updated by the computer department. Using the quality-to-
security tools, the project team conducted this information process risk
assessment at each step of lease application and subsequently secured
the entire process.

A KEY POINT

This actual case illustrates how important it is that the project team be composed of a cross-section of employees holding different job positions within the department: A single process, such as the above processing of an application through the leasing application department, may cut across several job positions. The key point is that employees closest to this process are those who perform the job tasks and therefore are also the employees who are the most knowledgeable about the sequence of tasks. These individuals also are in the best positions to identify weaknesses in the process and solutions to correct them.

THE PARETO ANALYSIS: DEFINITION, DESCRIPTION, AND ILLUSTRATION

DEFINING PARETO ANALYSIS

Pareto analysis is a problem-solving method developed in 1986 by Taguchi, a pioneer in the quality control movement, and adapted by the Business Information Security Program (BISP) for controlling security. Pareto analysis prioritizes problems identified in cause-and-effect analysis in their order of importance. The Pareto diagram is a simple bar chart that lists the frequencies of potential threats of a problem. For purposes of information process security, the place in the process having the most potential threats is also the most important problem and the first in order of priority to be secured.

DESCRIBING PARETO ANALYSIS

Consider a document that arrives at a company by the U.S. mail. The document is (1) delivered to the company mailroom, (2) sorted, (3) picked up by a mail clerk, (4) delivered to a departmental mailbox, and (5) retrieved by an employee or delivered to some job position where one or more job tasks are performed on the document. Examples of such tasks may be entering information into a company database or verifying information on the document. Typically, several job positions may perform several job tasks involving either paper or digital processing of incoming financial and other applications and documents. In this brief scenario, there are at least four susceptible points where the identity of an employee or customer could be compromised: (1) from the incoming company mailbox by anyone passing by, (2) by a mail clerk or someone impersonating a mail clerk, (3) by anyone who might see the document lying on a desk or displayed on a computer screen, or (4) by someone in the input-throughput-output chain of job positions where sequential tasks are performed on the document. This information process has, in great part, already been secured by securing the people front. However, to secure the process, information security requires a two-pronged approach—people and process security.

ILLUSTRATING THE PARETO DIAGRAM

To construct a Pareto diagram (Exhibit J.1), use a columnar pad to list the item to be secured and the locations in the process in which this item is susceptible to theft. Locations refer to the job tasks and/or the job positions that perform the tasks. Using the preceding example, in column 1 and on line 1 write "U.S. mail document." In columns 2 through 4, write down each of the four points in the process where the document or information from the document may not be secure: (2) delivery position (do not use names, only names of job tasks or job positions), (3) job task #1 (job position #1), (4) job task/position #2, and so on. Now place a check mark in each of the four columns, because, as described, each of the locations where the job task is performed is potentially unsecured.

Next, select another item that was identified in the brainstorming, built on in the cause-and-effect analysis, and visualized in the flow chart analysis. Perhaps, for example, the document containing employee or customer identities comes into the department as a fax copy. Again in column 1 and now in row 2, write "fax copy." Does the fax copy go to job task/position #1? If so, place a check mark in the third column, and so on.

For purposes of quality control, Pareto analysis can involve statistical analysis. For purposes of information process security, the statistics simply involve computing frequencies—the numbers of problems identified for each of the items in column 1. The items are to be ordered according to the highest frequency, that is, the locations having the most check marks. The last step is to prepare a bar chart to graphically illustrate this frequency distribution. (See Exhibits J.1 and J.2.)

EXHIBIT J.1   *Frequencies for Pareto Analysis*

Source to Be Secured	Delivery Position	Task/Position #1	Task/Position #2	F
U.S. mail document	X	X	X	3
Fax document		X	X	2

Note: X = Locations where a type of document is to be secured. For example, for documents that come into a department by U.S. mail, security may be necessary at three locations: the delivery desk, a sorting desk, and another desk where tasks may be performed on one type of document.

F = Frequencies or total number of locations (where job tasks are performed) to be secured.

<u>**EXHIBIT J.2**   *Bar Chart for Pareto Frequencies*</u>

Number of Locations

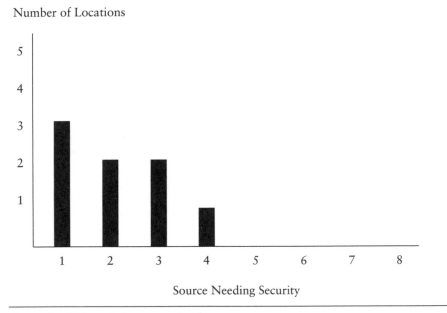

Source Needing Security

Key: 1 = U.S. mail document, 2 = fax, etc.

Note: Display the locations in the order of *descending* frequencies. On the graph, for example, for documents that come into a department by way of U.S. mail, three locations require security, and for fax documents, two locations require security.

FORERUNNERS IN THE SUPPORT OF IDENTITY THEFT LEGISLATION

U.S. SENATORS

U.S. Senator Barbara Allen, R-Kansas
E-mail: *allen@senate.state.ks.us*

U.S. Senator Joseph R. Biden, D-Delaware
E-mail: *senator@biden.senate.gov*

U.S. Senator Maria Cantwell, D-Washington
E-mail: Online form at *http://cantwell.senate.gov/contact/index.html*

U.S. Senator Mike DeWine, R-Ohio
E-mail: Online form at *http://www.senate.gov/~dewine/*

U.S. Senator Richard J. Durbin, D-Illinois
E-mail: *dick@durbin.senate.gov*

U.S. Senator Dianne Feinstein, D-California
E-mail: Online form at *www.senate.gov/~feinstein/email.html*

U.S. Senator Charles "Chuck" Grassley, R-Iowa
E-mail: *chuck_grassley@grassley.senate.gov*

U.S. Senator Judd Greg, R-New Hampshire
E-mail: *mailbox@greg.senate.gov*

U.S. Senator Orrin Hatch, R-Utah
E-mail: Online form at *www.senate.gov/~hatch/email_form.htm*

U.S. Senator Herbert Kohl, D-Wisconsin
E-mail: *senator_kohl@kohl.senate.gov*

U. S. Senator Jon Kyl, R-Arizona
E-mail: Online form at *www.senate.gov/~kyl/con_form.htm*

U.S. Senator Mitch McConnell, R-Kentucky
E-mail: *senator@mcconnell.senate.gov*

U.S. Senator Jeff Sessions, R-Alabama
E-mail: *senator@sessions.senate.gov*

U.S. Senator Arlen Specter, R-Pennsylvania
E-mail: Online email form at *www.senate.gov/~specter/webform.htm*

U.S. Senate Committee on the Judiciary
Subcommittee on Technology, Terrorism, and Government Information
224 Dirksen Senate Office Building
Washington, DC 20510
Majority Office Phone: (202) 224-5225
Majority Office Fax: (202) 224-9102
Republican Office Phone: (202) 224-6791
Republican Office Fax: (202) 228-0542
Web site: *http://judiciary.senate.gov/*

STATE OFFICIALS

Governor Jeb Bush
State of Florida
E-mail: Online form at *www.state.fl.us/eog/govmailform.html* or
       jeb.bush@myflorida.com

Attorney General Roy Cooper
State of North Carolina
North Carolina Attorney General's Office
E-mail: *agjus@mail.jus.state.nc.us*

Attorney General Drew Edmondson
State of Oklahoma
E-mail: Online form at *www.oag.state.ok.us/feedback.nsf/feedback*

Attorney General Christine O. Gregoire
State of Washington
E-mail: *ago@atg.wa.gov*

Attorney General Bill Lockyer
State of California
Web site: *http://caag.state.ca.us/ag/lockyer.htm*

Attorney General Bill Pryor
State of Alabama
Web site: *www.ago.state.al.us/*

Senator Pam Redfield, Nebraska
E-mail: *predfield@unicam.state.ne.us*

Attorney General Ken Salazar
State of Colorado
E-mail: *attorney.general@state.co.us*

Jim Tedisco, Assemblyman
New York State Assembly
E-mail: Online form at *http://assembly.state.ny.us/mem/?ad=103&sh=con*

State Attorney Jeff Tomczak
State of Illinois
E-mail: *StatesAttorney@willcountyillinois.com*

Stephen P. Weber, CPA
Will County, Illinois, Auditor
E-mail: *sweber@willcountyillinois.com*

OTHERS

Nedra Pickler, Associated Press Writer
E-mail: *npickler@ap.org*

Richard M. Stana
Director, Justice Issues
The United States General Accounting Office
Web site: *www.gao.gov*

Frank Torres, III
Legislative Counsel
Consumers Union (Washington, DC office)
E-mail: *Torrfr@consumers.org*

NOTES

Chapter 1

1. Committee on the Judiciary, House of Representatives, Joint Hearing, 107th Congress, Second Session, *Risk to Homeland Security from Identity Fraud and Identity Theft* (Washington, DC: U.S. Government Printing Office, June 25, 2002); J. Hudson, *ATM Skimming Funding Terrorists* (West Linn, OR: American Criminal Investigators Network, April 14, 2004); Dennis Lormel, "Combating Terror Financing in America," Special Policy Forum Report No. 867, *Policywatch* (Washington, DC: The Washington Institute, April 27, 2004); "Identity Theft Grows as Tool of Criminal, Terrorist Laundering," Moneylaundering.com (June 2004), *www.moneylaundering.com/ArticleDisplay.aspx?id=2955*; P. O'Carroll, "The Homeland Security and Terrorism Threat from Document Fraud, Identity Theft and Social Security Number Misuse," Congressional Testimony, U.S. Senate, Committee on Finance (Washington, DC: Office of the Inspector General, Social Security Administration, September 9, 2003); Department of the Treasury, "Treasury and Federal Financial Regulators Issue Final Patriot Act Regulations on Customer Identification," Press Release JS-335 (Washington, DC: Office of Public Affairs, April 30, 2003).
2. U.S. Department of Justice, *Al Qaeda Training Manual,* February 23, 2004, *www.usdoj.gov/ag/trainingmanual.htm.*
3. R. Pear, "Thousands Are Getting IDs Illegally," New York Times News Service, May 20, 2002, cached: *www.dallasnews.com/latestnews/stories/ 052002dnnatsocial.11b8f.html.*

Chapter 2

1. Judith M. Collins and Tracy McGinley, "Identity Theft Victims and the Process of Healing," Manuscript (2001), Michigan State University–Business Identity Theft Partnerships for Prevention, 540 Baker Hall, East Lansing, MI 48824-1118, available from Judith Collins, *judithc@msu.edu* or *idtheft@msu.edu.*

2. J.M. Collins and S.K. Hoffman, "Identity Theft: Predator Profiles. Based on 1,037 Actual Cases," Manuscript (2003), Michigan State University–Business Identity Theft Partnerships for Prevention, East Lansing, MI 48824-1118, available from Judith Collins, *judithc@msu.edu* or *idtheft@msu.edu*; Seth Stern, "Tougher Penalties for Identity Theft Win Approval from House Committee," *Congressional Quarterly–Legal Affairs* (May 12, 2004); Thomas Claburn, "Feds Want Tougher Penalties for Insider Identity Theft," *InformationWeek* (May 24, 2004), *www.informationweek.com/ shared/printableArticle.jhtml?articleID=20900519*; U.S. Senate, 108th Congress, Second Session, H.R. 1731, "An Act," Section 1028A(c) (Washington, DC: U.S. Government Printing Office, June 24, 2005); United States Secret Service and CERT Coordination Center (CERT/CC) of Carnegie Mellon University, "Survey of Network Security and Insider Threats" (2003/2004) available at *www.survey.cert.org/InsiderThreat*; Collins and McGinley, "Identity Theft Victims;" R. Pear, "Thousands Are Getting IDs illegally," *New York Times* News Service (May 20, 2002) cached: *http:// www.dallasnews.com/lastestnews/stories/052002dnnatsocial.11b8f. html*; R. Richardson, *Computer Security Institute/Federal Bureau of Investigation Computer Crime and Security Survey*, Computer Security Institute (2003), available from *rrichardson@cmp.com.*

3. The Identity Theft Resource Center is an online resource for victims of identity theft and can be found at *www.idtheftcenter.org.* The postal address is PO Box 26833, San Diego, CA 92196. Michigan State University–Business Identity Theft Partnerships for Prevention, 540 Baker Hall, Michigan State University, East Lansing, MI 48828-1118. Michigan State University Identity Theft Crime and Research Laboratory, 116 Baker Hall, Michigan State University, East Lansing, MI 48824-1118, *idtheft@msu.edu*, *www.cj.msu.edu/~outreach/identity.*

4. The Federal Trade Commission's identity theft help site is located at *www.consumer.gov/idtheft/.*

5. Tim McDonald, "Global Internet Banking Scam Closed, Investigators Say" (April 13, 2001), reported in *www.newsfactor.com/perl/ story/?id=8951.*

6. Liz Flynn, "New Identity Theft Scam," *Southeast NewsLeader* (Savannah, Georgia); (April 21, 2004), *www.wtoctv.com/global/story.asp?s=1804798&ClientType=Printable.*
7. "Ford Credit Warns Customers to Be Aware of Identity Theft" (May 16, 2002), *www.freep.com/news/statewire/sw55929_20020516.htm.*
8. "Oakland Briefs: Stolen Computer, Data Worries EDS" (May 20, 2002), *http://detnews.com/2002/oakland/0204/26/d04-475315.*
9. John Branton, "Stamping Out Mail Theft" (April 22, 2004), *www.columbian.com/04222004/neighbor/137598.html.*

Chapter 3

1. Health Insurance Portability and Accountability Act of 1996, Public Law 104-191, 104th Congress (Washington, DC: U.S. Government Printing Office, August 21, 1996), *www.hhs.gov/ocr/hipaa/.*

Chapter 4

1. J.M. Collins and S.K. Hoffman, "Identity Theft: Predator Profiles: Based on 1,037 Actual Cases" manuscript (2003), Michigan State University–Business Identity Theft Partnerships for Prevention, East Lansing, MI 48824-1118, available from Judith Collins, *judithc@msu.edu* or *idtheft@msu.edu*); Richard Girgenti, "KPMG Fraud Survey" (2003), contact: *www.kpmg.com*; Brian Burke, "IDC's Enterprise Security Survey," R104-14400 (December 2003), report available at *www.mindbvranch.com/listing/product/R104-14400.html*; interview with Howard Beales, III, reported by Margaret Kane, "Insiders Pose ID Theft Threat" (January 23, 2003), CNET News.com, available at *www.cnet.com*; Vericept, Webinar presentation, "Protecting Your Information and Reputation" (July 2003), discussion of Trans Union Report, *www.vericept.com*; R. Pear, "Thousands Are Getting IDs illegally," *New York Times* News Service, May 20, 2002, cached: *http://www.dallasnews.com/lastestnews/stories/052002dnnatsocial.11b8f.html*; R. Richardson, *Computer Security Institute/Federal Bureau of Investigation Computer Crime and Security Survey*, Computer Security Institute (2003), available from *rrichardson@cmp.com.*
2. *Victim's Report* (2003), Identity Theft Crime and Research Laboratory, School of Criminal Justice, Michigan State University, Baker Hall, East Lansing, MI 48824–1118, available at *idtheft@msu.edu.*
3. Ibid.

4. Ibid.
5. The Gramm-Leach-Bliley Act gives authority to eight federal agencies and the states to administer and enforce the Financial Privacy Rule (*www.ftc.gov/privacy/ privacyinitiatives/financial_rule.html*) and the Safeguards Rule. These two regulations apply to "financial institutions," which include not only banks, securities firms, and insurance companies, but also companies providing many other types of financial products and services to consumers. See *www.ftc.gov/privacy/gloats/*. Under the GLB Act, the Safeguards Rule, enforced by the Federal Trade Commission, requires financial institutions to have a security plan to protect the confidentiality and integrity of personal consumer information. See *www.ftc.gov/privacy/privacyinitiatives/*.
6. U.S. Senator Dianne Feinstein, *www.feinstein.senate.gov/IDTheft.htm*.
7. The Equal Employment Opportunity Commission Uniform Guidelines on fairness in personnel practices can be found online at *www.eeoc.gov/policy/regs/ind*; Title VII of the Civil Rights Act of 1964 (Public Law 88-352), amended by the Civil Rights Act of 1991 (Public Law 102-166) prohibiting employment discrimination, is enforced by the Equal Employment Opportunity Commission.

Chapter 5

1. The Fair Credit Reporting Act can be found at *www.ftc.gov/os/statutes/fcra.htm*; Federal Trade Commission, Financial Privacy Rule, *www.ftc.gov/privacy/privacyinitiatives/financial_rule.html*; financial institutions are regulated by numerous Federal Bank Regulatory agencies, including the U.S. Treasury's Office of the Comptroller of the Currency, Treasury (OCC), the Federal Reserve System's Board of Governors, Federal Deposit Insurance Corporation (FDIC), and the Office of Thrift Supervision, Treasury (OTS), collectively called the Federal Agencies; the Health Insurance Portability and Accountability Act can be found at *www.hhs.gov/ocr/hipaa*; the Safeguards Rule can be found at *www.ftc.gov/privacy/gloats/*.
2. Ibid.
3. Federal Trade Commission, Financial Privacy Rule.

Chapter 7

1. J.M. Collins and S.K. Hoffman, "Identity Theft: Predator Profiles. Based on 1,037 Actual Cases," Manuscript (2003), Michigan State

University–Business Identity Theft Partnerships for Prevention, East Lansing, MI 48824-1118, available from Judith Collins, *judithc@ msu.edu* or *idtheft@msu.edu*; Richard Girgenti, "KPMG Fraud Survey" (2003), contact: *www.kpmg.com*; Brian Burke, "IDC's Enterprise Security Survey," R104-14400 (December 2003), available at *www.mindbvranch.com/listing/product/R104-14400.html*; interview with Howard Beales, III, reported by Margaret Kane, "Insiders Pose ID Theft Threat" (January 23, 2003), CNET News.com, available at *www.cnet.com*; Vericept, Webinar presentation, "Protecting Your Information and Reputation" (July 2003), discussion of Trans Union Report, available at *www.vericept.com*. The Equal Employment Opportunity Commission Uniform Guidelines on fairness in personnel practices can be found online at *http://www.eeoc.gov/ policy/ regs/index.html*; R. Pear, "Thousands Are Getting IDs illegally," *New York Times* News Service, May 20, 2002, cached: *http:// www.dallasnews.com/lastestnews/stories/052002dnnatsocial.11b8f. html*; R. Richardson, *Computer Security Institute/Federal Bureau of Investigation Computer Crime and Security Survey*, Computer Security Institute (2003), available from *rrichardson@cmp.com*.

2. Title VII of the Civil Rights Act of 1964 (Public Law 88-352), amended by the Civil Rights Act of 1991 (Public Law 102-166) prohibiting employment discrimination, is enforced by the Equal Employment Opportunity Commission (EEOC), *www.eeoc.gov/policy/ regs/index.html*.

Chapter 8

1. These references describe the background and development of the *quality* management tools (formal brainstorming, cause-and-effect analysis, flow-charting, and Pareto analysis) that, in this book, are adapted to *security* management and used to complete the exercises throughout: Mary Walton, *The Deming Management Method* (New York: The Putnam Publishing Group, 1986); H. Gitlow, *Planning for Quality, Productivity, and Competitive Position* (Homewood, IL: Dow Jones-Irwin, 1990); H. Gitlow, S. Gitlow, A. Oppenheim, and R. Oppenheim, *Tools and Methods for the Improvement of Quality* (Homewood, IL: Dow Jones-Irwin, 1989); K. Isakawa, *Guide to Quality Control* (Hong Kong: Asian Productivity Organization, Nordica International Limited (1976, available in the United States from UNIPUB, New York); J.M. Juran, *Quality Control Handbook*, 3rd ed. (New York: McGraw-Hill, 1979);

Amitava Mitra, *Fundamentals of Quality Control and Improvement* (New York: Macmillan, 1993) (note: requires knowledge of statistics).

Chapter 9

1. The Equal Employment Opportunity Commission Uniform Guidelines on fairness in personnel practices can be found at *www.eeoc.gov/policy/regs/index.html.*

Chapter 11

1. Test fairness means the test must not discriminate among subgroups: gender, race, ethnicity, and others.
2. K. Geisinger, "Review of the Wonderlic Personnel Test and Scholastic Level Exam," in Barbara S. Plake, James C. Impara, and Linda L. Murphy, eds., *The Fourteenth Mental Measurements Yearbook,* pp. 1359–1363 (Lincoln, NE: The Buros Institute of Mental Measurements, University of Nebraska-Lincoln, 2001); F. L. Schmidt, "Review of the Wonderlic Personnel Test," in J.V. Mitchell Jr., ed., *The Ninth Mental Measurements Yearbook,* pp. 1755–1757 (Lincoln, NE: Buros Institute of Mental Measurements, University of Nebraska-Lincoln, 1985).

Chapter 12

1. H.G. Gough and P. Bradley, *California Psychological Inventory Manual,* 3rd ed. (Palto Alto, CA: Consulting Psychologists Press, 1996).

Chapter 13

1. H.G. Gough, "Theory, Development, and Interpretations of the CPI Socialization Scale," *Psychological Reports,* Suppl. 1-V75 (1994): 651–700.

Chapter 18

1. These references describe the background and development of the *quality* management tools (formal brainstorming, cause-and-effect

analysis, flow-charting, and Pareto analysis) that, in this book, are adapted to security management and used to complete the exercises throughout: Mary Walton, The Deming Management Method (New York: The Putnam Publishing Group, 1986); H. Gitlow, Planning for Quality, Productivity, and Competitive Position (Homewood, IL: Dow Jones-Irwin, 1990); H. Gitlow, S. Gitlow, A. Oppenheim, and R. Oppenheim, Tools and Methods for the Improvement of Quality (Homewood, IL: Dow Jones-Irwin, 1989); K. Isakawa, Guide to Quality Control (Hong Kong: Asian Productivity Organization, Nordica International Limited (1976; available in the United States from UNIPUB, New York); J.M. Juran, Quality Control Handbook, 3rd ed. (New York: McGraw-Hill, 1979); Amitava Mitra, Fundamentals of Quality Control and Improvement (New York: Macmillan, 1993) (note: requires knowledge of statistics).

Chapter 20

1. J.M. Collins and S.K. Hoffman, First Responders to Identity Theft: Police Officers, Prosecutors, and Judges (Flushing, NY: Looseleaf Law Publications, 2004).
2. J.M. Collins and T. McGinley, "Identity Theft Victims and the Process of Healing," Michigan State University–Business Identity Theft Partnerships in Prevention, East Lansing, MI 48824), 2001, judithc@msu.edu or idtheft@msu.edu.
3. J.M. Collins and S.K. Hoffman, Identity Theft Victims' Assistance Guide (Flushing, NY: Looseleaf Law Publications, 2004).

Chapter 22

1. Identity Theft and Assumption Deterrence Act of 1998, 105th Congress, Public Law 105-318, October 30,1998. Can be obtained at http://www.ftc.gov/.

Chapter 23

1. Health Insurance Portability and Accountability Act of 1996, Public Law 104-191, 104th Congress (Washington, DC: U.S. Government Printing Office, 1996), www.hhs.gov/ocr/hipaa/.
2. J.M. Collins and S.K. Hoffman, "Identity Theft: Predator Profiles, Based on 1,037 Cases," Michigan State University–Business Identity

Theft Partnerships in Prevention (East Lansing, MI 48824, 2003), *judithc@msu.edu* or *idtheft@msu.edu*.
3. *Health Insurance Portability and Accountability Act of 1996*, Public Law 104-191, 104th Congress (Washington, DC: U.S. Government Printing Office, 1996), *www.hhs.gov/ocr/hipaa/*.

Appendix C

1. See note 1 for Chapter 8.

INDEX